EVERY PENNY COUNTS

Practical Guide to Making More Money

Rudy Schmid, CPA

ISBN:

979-8-89669-006-1 (Paperback)

979-8-89669-007-8 (Hardcover)

Foreword

I will admit that the true inspiration for writing this book was the excitement of profits!

When we buy low and sell high, thereby earning a profit, it means we have reached our pinnacle in the commercial world! We have gone for the stars and reached them! It gives us an incredible feeling of accomplishment as we celebrate with our profits.

Of course, there are degrees of profits, and we might ask ourselves whether we could have earned even more, maybe 6% of sales rather than 5%. Could we have increased our sales, thereby causing our profit percentage to rise to greater levels? After all, 5% of $100,000 is so much more than 5% of $50,000. In other words, how much more can we do to cause our profits to increase to higher levels? What did Apple and Microsoft do to create such enormous profits? Those questions and our quest in searching for the answers have given us purpose and resolve in writing this book, appropriately named Every Penny Counts.

I want to explore beyond the basic ratios, into the makeup of each element of an Income Statement. I want to inquire about the level of sales, the amount and quality of promotion, direct advertising, and the selection of media to spread the word about the products. What methods are employed to create excitement in the consumer market? This, I believe, is where selling begins, as consumers learn about a product and eventually want it. When it arrives on the shelves, those same consumers are eagerly searching for it and ready to buy!

Next, as the developer, I want to dissect the product to be sold, for each element required to create it. Is my cost the lowest I can get, and at the best quality I can buy? Can I lower the cost by purchasing in greater quantities? Can my delivery costs be lower? All these questions about bringing my product to the market and selling larger quantities can be explored in detail. And, of course, executed with the best alternatives.

Finally, there are the numerous overhead expenses that must be paid from sales proceeds before final profits can be realized. Rental expenses, utilities, employee wages, payroll tax and so many more. Each expense element deserves a second look, the second being in greater detail to justify its existence. For example, business insurance can be given an in-depth study to ensure that policies will cover only what is needed and at the best premium. Transportation expense can be studied as to who is using company vehicles and for what purposes, to arrive at the most efficient usage. Each expense can be dissected for its content and scrutinized carefully. The final result can be a handful of reduced amounts that can combine with increased sales for potentially large savings. When those micro- studies, each with the goal of increasing sales while decreasing costs and overhead, have been carefully carried out, the result can be a dramatic increase in profits.!

This is the field of Every Penny Counts! The following pages are intended to serve as a guide for you along this exciting and lucrative path for your own company!

There are several memorandums and books written about maximizing profits. Some are helpful, while others are intangible and difficult to apply. It is with unbounded optimism that I decided to undertake the writing of a meaningful book, easy to understand and with suggested steps that will be easy to apply. These will be my objectives.

With decades of experience and practice in preparing and working with income statements, questions dealing with profit maximization have often entered my mind. Believing that, while a company reached profitable levels, why could it not be still better? The giants of industry have obviously reached profits far beyond amounts that were thought to be possible.

The giants in science, technology, and retail trades have found the secrets to unbelievable profits that were unknown in earlier years. Sales have sky-rocketed! Profits have soared, and for those recently beginning company ownership, I feel certain you will want to follow in their profitable footsteps. That is the simple reason why I have decided to write this book about Every Penny Counts I don't know all of the answers, but I have great confidence in being able to describe many of the steps taken, that will be a great help to you.

With all my best wishes for your success.

Rudy Schmid, CPA

Dedication

I am particularly excited and pleased to acknowledge my granddaughter and her husband, Kylie and Robert Simcox, for their exceptional accomplishments in forming and operating a company. Having started a business in specialty woodworking, known as WINDSET STUDIOS, they have applied principles of entrepreneurship and micro-profiting, earning a healthy profit in their first year, and their second!

I am so proud of their amazing business accomplishments!

Table of Contents

1

About the Author

Rudy Schmid, author of The Entrepreneur's Guide, has had a remarkable career spanning over six decades in the accounting profession. Initially struggling with math in school, his fascination with numbers led him to work harder and eventually gain a solid understanding of how to effectively manage finances. Rudy graduated from UCLA's Business School in 1958 and began his career with Ernst & Ernst (now Ernst & Young), where he honed his skills in auditing and developed a passion for providing constructive financial insights to businesses.

In 1960, Rudy started his own practice, Rudolf F. Schmid, CPA, in Santa Maria, California. Over the years, he provided services in accounting, income tax, and consulting to businesses across various industries. By 1968, he expanded his practice to Santa Barbara, where he also took on roles as a part-time controller for mid-sized companies. Rudy later ventured into software development, where he led a project to automate data processing in the airline industry, although the company eventually succumbed to competition due to limited capital.

Rudy's career took another turn in 1985 when he became a controller for a multi-company organization in Baltimore. His work in cattle raising, dairy farming, grain farming, and real estate development included managing finances for a $250 million residential community project. His ability to present financial reports in a meaningful way was highly valued, and it inspired him to write The Entrepreneur's Guide.

Throughout his 64-year career as a Certified Public Accountant, Rudy worked in nearly every business sector and continued in his role as a controller until his retirement in 2022, at the age of 90. Rudy believes that accounting, far from being boring, is an exciting and fulfilling profession that directly impacts a company's success.

Now 92, Rudy is a proud father of seven children, grandfather to thirteen, and great-grandfather to eight. He lives in Sykesville, Maryland, and enjoys good health.

Page Blank Intentionally

1

Before Micro-profits

Quality Accounting and Reporting

The topic of micro-accounting and micro-profiting is exciting to imagine, even with the smallest entrees making a critical difference. Reclassifying an entry or correcting a misclassified account will be the area of our search. Making such entries suggests the importance of quality from the ground up, beginning with the classification of accounts and the inclusion of all-important amounts. I also suggest that changes in the "Micro" phase become almost meaningless until earlier corrections have been made. For this reason, I believe it is highly important that we first discuss the measures taken by the accounting profession to ensure quality in standards of accounting and preparation of financial statements. After describing the measures taken to ensure quality reporting, we will move to the exciting phase of micro-profits.

Accepted Accounting Principles and Reporting Standards.

The recognition of quality financial information dates to the early nineteenth Century, a time when the industrial revolution was a growing movement. It was a time when large corporations desperately sought to attract investors. Reliance upon quality data led to the focus on trained accountants, which in turn led to the formation in 1887 of the institute that grew to become the American Institute of Certified Public Accountants. The primary focus of the organization was to formulate quality principles of accounting and uniform standards of reporting, upon which readers and potential investors could rely.

It led to the formation of the American Financial Standards Board (AFSB), that established rules, standards and procedures. They become known as:

"Generally Accepted Accounting Principles" (GAAP). Today, GAAP is accepted and followed by public companies throughout the United States, as well as by governmental agencies. The establishment and wide acceptance of GAAP has resulted in formal standards that require financial statements to be prepared in a complete form, and in a consistent manner, allowing for comparable analysis.

In a broader scope, while GAAP is used in the United States, most other countries follow the International Financial Reporting Standards (IFRS). However, as the world is becoming smaller, active steps are underway to unify the two sets of standards. Today, the AICPA comprises a membership of close to one-half million members, each of whom has passed strict requirements and been licensed as Certified Public Accountants. It is the accountant's responsibility to abide by GAAP when providing services to clients, including the preparation of financial statements. If there are any departures from GAAP, it is to be noted in the statements.

The importance of using GAAP in financial reporting applies to all publicly traded stocks. Each of those companies must follow rules that have been established by the Securities Exchange Commission (SEC) and those rules include adherence to GAAP. Today the rules of GAAP have become so widely known and accepted in the business world that most non-public companies also follow them.

Audits!

The word "Audit" may remind us of actions by the Internal Revenue Service, but it is equally utilized throughout the business world to ensure quality in reporting and compliance with established accounting rules. Audits are conducted by Certified Public Accountants and can be described as the examination of detailed financial accounting records, searching for compliance with GAAP and proper reporting. When errors are found, "audit adjustments" are made and audited financial statements are prepared.

The most vital and meaningful step at the conclusion of an audit is the preparation of an "opinion letter," in which the CPA states that the reports "fairly present" the condition of the company for the period audited. With the words "fairly present" in the letter, the reports are normally accepted by the audited company. With the audit letter, the company can confidently present financial reports to its Board of Directors, investors, potential investors and creditors.

In short, the quality of accounting and reporting has become uniformly accepted and adhered to throughout the fifty states, providing a high level of confidence in the numbers.

2

Micro-profiting

Having established a level of quality in the numbers, we can now move into the exciting area of Micro-profiting! This is where we can work with numbers, knowing that any changes made will be in the creation of final figures to be reported.

Imagine that you begin a new company with the intention of becoming large and profitable. You plan for it to grow over time into a highly successful business, just as Microsoft did in the 1970s, beginning with its first computer sale, and one day becoming the world's wealthiest company.

Everyone can have the same dream, and if you have a product that will be welcomed in the marketplace and take the right steps, you too might achieve your dreams. The questions are: what are those steps? Industry giants like Apple, Inc., General Motors, and Standard Oil took them just as thousands of other companies that operate successfully. The answers to success, however, can often become complex, overlooked, and not always easy to find.

To be profitable means to sell a product for a price that, when diminished by its cost and expenses in operating the business, leaves a sufficient amount remaining, which is the net profit.

For example, you purchase an item for $40.00 and sell it for $100.00, leaving a healthy gross profit of $60.00. When other necessary expenses are paid, like rent, utilities and a few others, amounting to $35.00 per unit, a healthy net profit remains of $25.00. When more of the products are sold, the $25.00 net profit is multiplied with each sale. When not allowing either the product cost or the operating expenses to grow out of control, the company can grow successfully.

Micro-profiting was designed to ensure that an awareness of the facts can always exist, allowing for remedial steps to be taken when necessary. As the owner, your steps might be one, or a combination of the following:

Raise the selling price or Take steps to lower the product cost and/or the operating expenses.

Our goal in Micro-profiting is to make the facts known as soon as possible – ASAP, allowing steps to be taken to keep profits on track and build the successful company of your dreams. On the following pages, we will look into the basics, what is meant by micro-profiting, and how it can be used to improve the product's quality and profitability.

3

The Basics

We will start at the very beginning of a business transaction, that is, to purchase a product for resale. This is where we will begin to plan for profit on the sale.

Step One– Purchasing the product:

Let's say the product cost $100. We decided to plan for a healthy gross profit when it is sold, so we selected 60%. If the cost of $100 is to generate a 60% profit, then it follows that the purchase cost must be 40%. To determine the selling price, divide 40 by 100, and it results in 250. To prove the result, we can add the cost and resulting profit of 150 to agree with the price of 250.

The following illustrates the resulting numbers of the products we purchased:

Step two – Establishing the Selling Price:

Divide the Purchase cost by 40% giving a Selling Price of	$250.00	100%
When subtracting Cost OF	100.00	40
Leaves a Gross Profit of	$150.00	60%

Step three – Distributing Overhead Expense:

Now it is time to focus on the Operating Expenses, also referred to as Overhead. All of the expenses of rent, utilities and others necessary to operate the business must be covered by gross profit. Good planning requires sales to cover overhead **and** leave a remaining balance as company profit.

Your Company Name
Income Statement
Year Ended December 31, 2023

	Percent-of Sales	Budget		% of Sales	Adjusted	
Revenue						
Sales			100,000.00			100,000.00
Cost of Sales:						
Beginning inventory	7.00	7,000.00		7.00	7,000.00	
Materials	13.00	13.000.00		10.00	10,000.00	
Labor	17.00	17,000.00		17.00	17,000.00	
Direct overhead	8.00	8,000.00		6.00	6,000.00	
Total	45.00	45,000.00		40.00	40,000.00	
Less End. Inventory	-5.00	(5,000.00)		(0.05)	(5,000.00)	
Cost of sales	40.00		40,000.00	0.35		35,000.00
Gross Profit	60.00		60,000.00	60.00		65,000.00
Operating Overhead:						
Rent	8.000	8,000.00		0.08	8,000.00	
Utilities	2.000	2,000.00		2.0	2,000.00	
Insurance	2.000	2,000.00		2.0	2,000.00	
Wages	11.000	11,000.00		10.0	10,000.00	
Payroll taxes	2.000	2,000.00		1.9	1,900.00	
Telephone/comp	1.000	1,000.00		1.9	1,000.00	
Transportation	2.000	2,000.00		1.8	1,800.00	
Advertising	4.000	4,000.00		4.0	4,000.00	
Repairs & maint.	2.000	2,000.00		2.0	2,000.00	
Depreciation	1.000	1,000.00		1.0	1,000.00	
Total Optg. Overhead	35.00	35,000.00	35,000.00	26.68	33,700.00	33,700.00
Net Operating Profit	25.00		25,000.00	33.32		31,300.00

Comments: While only a few changes are shown above for illustrative purposes. It is recommended that each cost and expense element be studied closely, in search of improvement. Question the fairness of allocations, the source of costs and expenses, and the possibility of alternative sources that could improve the bottom line. This is the heart of micro profiting, where time can be well invested to locate the best combinations of resources at the most efficient cost.

The question of how much overhead is to be charged against a sales category can be answered by the relationship of expenses to sales. We can support the rational by considering that it was not for the facilities to support operating the company. There could be no sales.

If only one product were sold by the company, then 100% of the expense would be deducted from total sales, with no requirement to allocate. However, when there are more products, then the need to allocate to each category of sales is required. Relative sales volumes appear to be the fairest method. Here is an example reporting one-month sales:

	Sales	Overhead Expense Distribution
Product 1	$ 40,000	40%
Product 2	20,000	20%
Product 3	15,000	15%
Product 4	20,000	20%
Product 5	5,000	5&
	Total: $100,000	100%

Step Four – Profit on Sales:

Let's carry our example to the final profit. Assume Product 1, with sales for the month of $40,000 and cost of the product at 40 percent of sales, or $16,000, leaving a Gross Profit of $24,000.

Assume a total Overhead of $50,000, of which 40%, or $20,000, is allocated to Product 1. Subtracting $20,000 from a Gross Profit of $24,000 leaves a Net Profit of $4,000 for the month for Product 1.

In the next Chapter, we will look into true micro-profiting, by looking closely at each cost element when manufacturing is involved, and the elements that comprise overhead. By doing this, we will gain even greater insight and the opportunity to improve and control the smallest details.

4

A Closer look at Cost and Overhead:

In Chapter Two, we looked at the purchased cost of a single product when merchandise was simply bought and resold. There are also conditions when a product is manufactured, requiring two or more cost elements to make up a complete product before being sold.

Imagine, for a moment, the construction of a new road, under contract with a county or state. There will be initial surveying, office work to develop plans, clearing, and finally, building the road with labor and equipment. In each phase of work, the opportunity exists to improve efficiency, lower costs and gain a more cost-effective project. Following the initial creation of a budget, closer studies can be conducted, resulting in combined improvement. A clear possibility exists for substantially increasing the final net profit.

Overhead:

Using the same approach to examine operating expenses, a closer look at each category can often lead to improvement of the data. Alternatives in the use of manpower or supplies may lead to greater efficiency. At a later date during the project, experience may lead to deletions or adjustments of certain expenses. This is the opportunity to take a second and third look to find ways to improve, or in the case where overruns are found, to locate the reasons and apply remedies.

The use of Percentages:

An important tool when analyzing costs and expenses is the use of a **Percent of Sales** for each element. For example, when the initial budget is prepared, reporting 5% of sales for a certain expense. It is later found to be double that amount and there is an immediate alarm to look closely for reasons and to take remedial action. By a frequent review of this "microdata," major problems can be located and solved early, saving the project and protecting profits.

Although the percentages might be calculated with Total Cost or Total Expense as the base, I prefer the use of Total Sales as the base. I believe this approach shows a more consistent relevance throughout a statement, and minimizes the possibility of confusion in reading a statement. To clarify, if Total Sales is used as the base of all percentages in the Statement, it can be read with greater understanding and meaning.

On the following page, a sample of the Income Statement is shown, with percentages originally shown per budget and also adjusted to point out differences.

Your Company Name
Income Statement
Year Ended December 31, 2023

Description	Budget	Percent of Sales	Adjusted	% of Sales
Revenue:				
Sales	100,000.00		100,000.00	
Cost of Sales:				
Beginning Inventory	7,000.00	7.0%	7,000.00	7.0%
Materials	13,000.00	13.0%	10,000.00	10.0%
Labor	17,000.00	17.0%	17,000.00	17.0%
Direct Overhead	8,000.00	8.0%	6,000.00	6.0%
Total	45,000.00	45.0%	40,000.00	40.0%
Less Ending Inventory	(5,000.00)	(5.0%)	(5,000.00)	(5.0%)
Cost of Sales	40,000.00	40.0%	35,000.00	35.0%
Gross Profit	60,000.00	60.0%	65,000.00	65.0%
Operating Overhead:				
Rent	8,000.00	8.0%	8,000.00	8.0%
Utilities	2,000.00	2.0%	2,000.00	2.0%
Insurance	2,000.00	2.0%	2,000.00	2.0%
Wages	11,000.00	11.0%	10,000.00	10.0%
Payroll Taxes	2,000.00	2.0%	2,000.00	2.0%
Telephone/Communications	1,000.00	1.0%	1,000.00	1.0%
Transportation	4,000.00	4.0%	4,000.00	4.0%
Advertising	2,000.00	2.0%	2,000.00	2.0%
Repairs & Maintenance	3,000.00	3.0%	3,000.00	3.0%
Depreciation	2,000.00	2.0%	2,000.00	2.0%
Total Operating Overhead	35,000.00	35.0%	34,000.00	34.0%
Net Operating Profit	25,000.00	25.0%	31,000.00	31.0%

Comments:

While only a few charges are shown for illustrative purposes, it is recommended that each cost and expense element be studied closely in search of improvement. Questions should be raised about the fairness of allocations, the source of costs and expenses, and the possibility of alternative sources that could improve the bottom line. This is the heart of micro-profiling, where time can be well-invested to identify the best combinations of resources at the most efficient cost.

5

Searching for the Profits!

It is like driving a car – we know where we want to go, but we need to watch closely to monitor the direction, speed, and other issues that may arise along the way, in order to finally reach our target successfully. Likewise, every company, large or small, should have goals, daily goals, weekly, monthly and annual, to work toward. They serve as guideposts to measure degrees of success, and to celebrate when met or exceeded. In support of goals, continued monitoring along the way provides us with updates on progress, and, equally, if not more important, with an opportunity to apply our controls. They would be a check on Total Sales, Gross Profit, and Net Profit. Let's look at some useful monitoring tests we can apply.

Gross sales: The single measurement of gross sales will tell us whether we are on track to meet or exceed our goals. Knowing our results to date can serve as an incentive to keep up the pace, work harder, or make a few strategic changes in our marketing plans. Consider tracking the progress of competition, and if the data is available, it is also helpful to be aware of your relative position in the marketplace. The best yet is to discover that you are number one in competitive sales and to take all steps to maintain it.

Gross Profit: So very important! We want to be aware at all times of our gross profit, that is, gross sales less product costs. If, for example, a 60% gross profit margin was initially established, material and labor costs may have risen, resulting in a corresponding decrease in gross profit. Daily or weekly monitoring of sales and cost data will tell the story. What do you do if your position is slipping?

First, you will want to go to direct costs of materials and labor. Have your costs increased recently? Go to the sources – your suppliers, and negotiate prices. If necessary, check with alternate suppliers for improved prices and terms.

Next, study your own employee records for labor allocations to the project. Have additional employees been added, or has overtime occurred? Make decisions based upon your most recent data. When your best decisions have been executed, the results of your findings and changes may indicate a price increase should be made to maintain your gross profit margin.

Operating Expenses: Your next step will be to re-examine each operating element. Review percentages of gross sales for each expense element. Consider steps to look deeply into the source and content of each one. Those steps might result in:

1. Reducing any labor that may be considered excessive. It could include discussions with employees regarding the reduction of overtime or the increase in efficiency.
2. Reconsider the extent of some expenses, like advertising, for example. Reduce to a lower percent of sales, also compare actual results to date relative to the initial budget. Take similar steps with each budgeted expense.

When a review of overhead is completed, additional decisions may be required to adjust selling prices in order to insure profitable net income.

3. In summary, to have a working plan for micro profiting means to:
   a. Establish sales goals, at least monthly and annually.

b. Apply inspection tests of sales, gross profit, and operating expenses frequently.

c. Take action steps to lower cost and expense elements, and

d. Adjust selling price accordingly to maintain pre-established profit margins.

6

Analyzing for Micro-profits!

The first thing we want to do in a new business is to sell our products and services. The second thing is to measure our progress against projections. This is the beginning of the analysis or the study of what happened when we had our first sale.

Why is it so important to study our progress? Why do we need it? I believe the most important reason is that having invested our time and money into the venture, we expect to earn a profit.

Now we want to know if we earned a profit, and if so, how much. That is the nature of business, and even a measure of good business management. Let's look at an example: Let's say we invested $100 to purchase a product for resale and sold it for $150,00. We just earned a Gross Profit on the sale of $50,00. But wait! There were expenses of packaging and shipping of $20.00 and the expense of utilities, insurance and wages of $60.00, showing that we actually lost $30.00 on the sale. This is just a simple example of the study of, or analysis of, the numbers that will reveal to us the real facts.

Over time, several key ratios and tests have been developed that allow us to learn if and how much of a profit or loss occurred in our business sales. When we know and understand these tests, it enables us to take remedial steps when needed, and to plan for earning even greater profits when key steps are taken. In the following pages, let's take a look at these meaningful tests:

Sales: While we know the amount of sales is not a ratio, or even a test, it is the starting point upon which we will measure results. Understandably, without sales we have nothing, but with our first sales, things begin to happen, with the sky is the limit!

We can use our Sales figures to compare with projections, or with past periods. If we discover that our sales for the month of January, for example, are ten percent higher than those of January one year ago, the increase will become very meaningful and encouraging. If we discover it is ten percent less it tells us that we need to look deeper for the reasons. "Sales" is where it all begins.

Gross Profit is the amount remaining after subtracting the direct cost of the product we sold.

If our business is retail sales, we can look at the cost of the product we just sold, subtracting it from its sale, and the remainder is our Gross Profit. If our business is manufacturing, we need to also look at the direct labor involved and other items required to build completed products. A Selling Price is often established by starting with the total direct cost and using it to arrive at a selling price that will create a certain Gross Profit. Let's look at an example. If we purchased a product for 100.00 and want to earn a gross profit of 60%, then by dividing our cost by .40 (the amount that will leave .60 as gross profit), we will calculate a selling price of $250.00.

We should also keep in mind that by dividing any cost or expense in our business by gross sales, we will learn its relative percent of sales. If, for example, we want to know the percent rent is to sales, wages, or taxes, simply divide the number by gross sales to find out. Further, by using the results to compare with prior and future periods, we begin to see trends that will give us encouraging results or reasons for concern. These are facts that become vital to business management and micro-profiting.

Net Profit is the bottom line, also referred to as Net Income, that reveals the amount of profit we earn after all costs and expenses have been deducted from sales.

While the Gross Profit figure tells us the profit level with only direct material and labor costs deducted, Net Profit is the next level after reducing Gross Profit by rents, wages, payroll taxes, utilities and all other overhead expenses required to operate the company. These expenses are referred to as Operating Expenses or as Overhead. The beauty of this group of expenses is that many of them remain at the same level without regard to the volume of sales. Rent, for example, will no doubt remain the same whether selling one hundred or one thousand units.

Inventory Turnover can be the path to dynamic growth in profits. It occurs when products are sold and more are purchased for sale. An example would be if one unit of a product were bought for $100.00 and sold for $250.00, earning a gross profit of $150.00. If ten units were bought and sold for the same price, a gross profit of $1,500.00 would be earned. It is simply the number of times we sell a product and earn a profit on it. We are simply turning over inventory with each sale.

We can determine our inventory turnover by dividing the Cost of Sales by Inventory over a given period of time, like a month, and the result should be the number of times inventory turned over during that time period. The more we can do it, the more our profits will soar.

7

Sales and more

When you have your first sale, life really begins for your company! It is the reason you invested your time, money and thoughts, and a great time to celebrate!

However, it won't be long before your business mind will begin to ask a few vital questions, like:

- How many more can I sell?
- What can I do to help sell more?
- If I take steps to help sell more units, what will it cost?
- What is my risk?
- Will the added cost be worth the increase in sales?

These are all valid questions, each deserving an answer. Not a quick response to finish the subject, but one that reflects the possibility of alternate materials, new ideas and consequences. If you spend more money on failed attempts, you could end up with a loss on your initial sale. So, you need to think the marketing process through from beginning to end and make your choices with great care. Let's look at a real product that sold big last year:

Is it a new idea that you will bring to the market? If it is, you will need to describe it very carefully, and explain why it is such a good item. Think for a moment of the electric car that entered the market in 2022 and 23. There had to be dozens of questions from buyers when they were not just buying another car but an electric car. "Why electric" for starters? What are the advantages of fuel-type cars? Better mileage? Lower expenses to operate? Does it cost more or less than a comparable fuel-driven car? How about refueling stations? Apparently, there were acceptable replies to the questions, as about 1.2 million electric cars were sold in the U.S. in 2023. What did Tesla and the other car dealers do to sell that many, especially when they were new to the market? Research tells us that Tesla spent about $152,000 on advertising, but Ford spent $370 million! If that seems high, consider that Toyota spent around $1.2 Billion and General Motors slightly higher. Why is there such a huge disparity in spending? These are questions that a marketing specialist must attempt to answer, but there is no doubt that marketing budgets are taken seriously. When you have a product that needs introduction to the marketplace or is very large, such as vehicles, a marketing specialist is needed.

Promotion and advertising come in many forms and deserve a vast amount of attention to bring expected sales results. Note the many talk shows on radio and TV, and the interviews that product representatives bring to these shows. It is one of the best methods of promoting sales, due to exposure to a captive audience and also minimum costs of being on the program.

- There are newspapers and magazine ads, direct advertising, and direct mail ads, to mention a few ways to spread the word about your product. My point is,
- Promotion and advertising are vitally important to the sale of a product, especially when dealing with a new idea or new item.
- The importance of this area will, in most instances, merit the use of a marketing specialist to help evaluate its features, and to build a program around the product and the particular market for which it is intended.

- Work closely with a specialist to design a program that utilizes available sources and methods of advertising within the available budget.
- Decide how long to run promotion and advertising programs.
- Keep in mind how important advertising is to the success of a sales program, and utilize available funds in careful ways, but not in excess of the budget.
- Keep a close watch over the promotion and advertising programs, comparing activities and costs with current sales.

In summary, I see promotion as letting as many potential consumers as possible know that you have the product, at a good price, the benefits it provides, and its ease to acquire. Get the word out as often as possible to those who might be the best potential buyers and at the lowest cost. Repeat the information as often as possible, within your budget.

When your marketing program is alive and well, product sales will be most likely to follow.

8

Revenue and Expenses

a. Sales

Let's say that your product is selling well and your company is earning a profit of nearly 10 percent of sales. "Not bad," you say, but you want to see a serious increase in sales and in the bottom line of your income statement. A Net Profit beyond 10%, and closer to 15% would be more acceptable to you and your shareholders.

The advertising budget has increased over the past year, pushing sales slightly upward but at a decreasing rate. In fact, you are getting a lesser return for each dollar spent on promotion and advertising than in the prior year. What can we do about it? How can we inject the market with new feelings of excitement, causing our sales to rise?

Okay, let's create ways to make it happen! Let's think "outside the box," as they say. There are methods that have proven to be successful, so we want to know about them. Here are a few that may work for you.

Rebranding:

This is a new way to sell your product that could mean a new life if done correctly. It could reach out to new markets, reaching new potential buyers. Here is what happens. It deals with looking at your present product in new ways. Coca-Cola did it a few years ago with great success. The product was already successful, selling world-wide – as the drink that satisfies. In 1985, a new Coke can was designed and placed on the market. It had a new appeal to the younger population, boosting sales dramatically. One might ask why a can could make such a difference?

We must realize that the market as a whole is a very emotional buyer. Appearance counts with most items we buy, like a certain look about the automobile that we drive or the furniture we place in our living room. Over time, buyers feel a genuine connection with certain products, a feeling that brings them back to shop for more. So, we cannot tamper too severely with the products we sell., unless it is clearly a positive change.

Around 2016, Coca-Cola began a campaign called "Taste the Feeling!" that only enhanced the product that had been already selling well. Recently, the Company added variations of the original – not, however, in place of the original - with Diet Coke and Coke Zero. They stressed added benefits while tasting as good as the Coke their customers had been enjoying for years. Each of the changes enhanced the original, thereby widening the market to include the younger generation and the diet continues. They were well thought out changes, built on, but not changing the original.

Let's look for a moment at Apple. We can recall in the 1970's, how the company awakened the world to the exciting personal computer. It was an immediate success everywhere! Not long after, Apple Computer, Inc. dropped the word "computer" from its name, and it was thereafter known as Apple, Inc. The Company was already well known and accepted in the marketplace for its computers, but with its new, all-encompassing name, it easily spread its brand to include the iPhone, iPad, etc. Apple was using its good reputation to apply to new products, which was worth its weight in gold. There was no need to start all over in promoting the new product names since they already carried the good name of Apple.

These two examples of rebranding both tell the same story of building upon the success of original products. It is important to remember this very important step when rebranding, that is, to not change your original product and the success it has enjoyed, but to build upon it, maintaining and enhancing the emotional connections that have been created.

New product:

This method of increasing sales can best be described by the new car industry. A certain brand, whether Ford, Chevy, or Toyota, redesigns its product, actually, several models of its brand with new lines, a few new features, and upgrades from the previous year, and sells them each year with exciting new promotions. In other words, they are new annual products, yet they are still Fords, Chevys, and Toyotas. The idea is that if you like your present model, you will surely like your new model even better. The technology in most years is the same, but with new tweaks and redesigns. Over the years, this program has been expected by the public, and in most cases, it has resulted in customers returning to buy the latest model. As to manufacturing costs, the machinery is already in the factory, with only minor adjustments needed each year, thereby reducing manufacturing costs. It is a program that is accepted in the marketplace and has worked quite well in most years to support sales.

Accessories:

This approach to increasing sales depends largely upon your original product. Is it a complete product with no need for additions, such as batteries? Toys that require batteries are great examples. An electric toothbrush is another. This is the type of thought that might be applied to building sales.

Multiple products:

When you reach a degree of success with product number one, measured by growing monthly sales that indicate market acceptance, consider a second and even a third product.

Consider that having conquered the hurdles of manufacturing and initial marketing of product Number one, you have paved the way for future products. They may use the available planning and engineering facilities, similar marketing methods, and similar delivery channels.

Executing these steps has already proven to be successful, as indicated by steady sales growth.

This may be the right time to pose the question, "Why not offer products 2 and maybe 3?

Developing and marketing the initial product was obviously, a pioneering undertaking, but market acceptance has proven it to be right for your company. As an example of adding products, think of Stanley Black & Decker Co., a tool company formed by the merger of Stanley Tools and Black & Decker, that has developed and marketed every imaginable tool, from a hammer to a tape measure. They were able to utilize the same equipment and marketing methods with each new product. As a result, the cost of sales proved to decrease with each new product, resulting in greater gross profits. A detailed study of your present product, together with the addition of another product or two, may prove to be a key to increased profits.

More about Sales!

A study of Sales can be the most exciting of all numbers in your company, because it represents so much to the company's very existence. The product you sell maybe your original idea and reason for going into business. It represents the very lifeblood of your company, probably like the cellphone to Apple, Inc. At any rate, sales are the starting point of everything in your company, the beginning of profits and growth of your company.

We are not only interested in the fact that there are sales, but in the volume. A study may find that they range anywhere between "pathetic" and "explosive." They, of course, deserve the greatest amount of attention, care, and thought to ensure continued growth.

To assist in maximizing sales, the following recommendations are offered:

Promotion:

When starting your new company, it is important to realize that potential customers do not know your company or your product. To remedy that condition, a carefully planned and executed campaign of promotion is vital. It is developed by reviewing and considering the use of numerous ways to introduce your product.

The best way to begin is to determine the type of customers that will most likely be interested in your product, that would have use for it and could best afford it. Money is wisely spent when reaching your target customers. The next question will be where to spend your promotion budget, such as:

- Radio – it is a good method for a wide audience, but not for a target audience.
- TV – Same as radio
- Direct mail: This method may be the most cost-effective, by mailing directly to your target group. It can be enhanced by including such items as:
- A discount coupon
- A 2-for-1 offer
- Sample of the product
- A special introductory offer.
- A guaranteed return offer if not 100% satisfied.
- Drawings for a prize, preferably where the potential winner enters their address data.
- Grand Opening
- Newspaper ads
- Website

Self-promotion: By personally meeting potential customers through trade shows, fairs, and other public places, you can add credibility to your product and company.

Consider Relocating: Considering the markets you intend to reach, are you located in the best place to reach your goals? What is the population of a potential market size?

Answers to these questions might suggest moving to an area of greater potential. Imagine for a moment that your new company is located in a "business friendly" city, where incentives are provided when you move there. Low income tax rates and preferred zoning, where city leadership welcomes you on arrival. You would clearly be off to a great start. Cincinnati, OH is one of those regions.

Imagine, too, that geographically you are located within easy reach of large market areas in which to sell your product; also, that transportation is close by, including major trucking, rail, air and even shipping facilities. Finally, imagine that you will be helped when employing needed workers through local job assistance agencies. All the support is needed to sell and fulfill the delivery of your product. All imaginable support is available to begin your company and realize growth at a healthy rate.

Commercial-friendly communities exist throughout the United States, offering tempting options for locating in an area most favorable to your needs, all with the ultimate goal of building sales for greater profits.

Specials:

Creating special sale events may reward you with the most return for dollars spent, for it is a great opportunity to call attention to your company and its products.

Events like Easter specials, Memorial Day and Labor Day are commonly used to sell products. During those Specials, greater discounts and lower prices are offered. You may prefer your own time of the year or the month to have your "Special" by prior planning, radio and TV interviews might be excellent ways to interact with potential customers, discussing all of the events and lower prices to be available.

Details of opportunities, like "2 for 1" sales, contests, and support of charities can be mentioned to help boost sales to record highs during that event.

Mergers:

Occasionally it happens that two companies have similarities that combining efforts would be beneficial to both.

An example is Black & Decker and Stanley tools. Both companies had earned success on their own, establishing strong reputations for quality products. By merging the companies, management determined that by reducing duplications in production and marketing, they were able to market their products more effectively and combine operating activities, resulting in greater profits.

Opportunities of this type are not always available, and if they are, it is of vital importance that management is compatible. There should be mutual agreement on short-term and long-term goals, also on product quality and marketing approach, along with leadership decisions. If not addressed early, disagreements will surely arise later, which must be avoided by early discussions. When agreement is reached on all of the key subjects, a merger could be an excellent path to greater profits.

Extended markets:

A company may be formed in a geographic location in the country, and operate there for no other reason but that the founders live there. In time, studies may reveal that the product would be very popular in another area. By a study of additional delivery costs and other related factors, management may find that expansion of the market area would greatly enhance product sales.

A few years ago I was associated as the accountant with a company that had developed a salad dressing. They tested the dressing locally with excellent response for one year. Following their test period, management associated with a national distributor. Within months, it grew to become a national best-seller. Management had started carefully to test market acceptance and iron out new product wrinkles. Once quality was confirmed, it stepped up to enjoy great increases in profits.

Other ways to boost sales:

A final approach to building sales in your company is to begin a program of revenue building. Imagine the department managers and the General Manager forming a committee that met monthly. They bring ideas to each meeting for presentation and discussion. Bonuses would be awarded for ideas that are accepted. The goals include "thinking outside the box" and brain-storming. Present the top ideas to the CEO for presentation at Board meetings.

A final thought is to form a partnership, a separate entity with certain standout employees who demonstrate their ability to think productively and willingness to work with new product development. The results may be amazing, leading to Micro-profiting!

b. Direct Material and Direct Labor Costs

This area includes all materials used to bring a product to "Finished" quality, ready for sale. If purchased for resale, it may include only the single purchase price, but if shipping and handling are separately charged, they should be included. When a product is manufactured, it is a different story, with perhaps dozens of items required to bring it to a finished product. When materials are initially gathered or listed for inclusion in a product, cost may not always be given top priority. But a review, or "second look" will provide the opportunity to look closely at each item. This time, the goal will be to search for several ways to improve, not only the cost, but through alternative materials, search for improved terms of purchase and possibly improved delivery timing. Each item should be given close scrutiny for improvement. Imagine the combined improvement when all direct parts are reviewed in this way!

Negotiations with suppliers may result in a number of improvements, including cost, terms and timing. In short, by focusing on each item that comprises a single product, improvements are likely to be found. That result, combined with similar results of all other parts, is the definition of micro-profiting!

Direct Labor:

A closer study of personnel assigned to handling or building a product can often bring rich rewards by lowering the total cost. Preparing a Job Description for each position involved will be the best method to control and evaluate direct labor costs. Each step needed in the process to bring a product to "finished" condition can be identified and assigned to an individual. By this method, each step can be clearly seen and understood. In doing so, fewer personnel may be required. Even more importantly, it will result in greater preparedness and efficiency.

In addition to direct labor costs, associated costs of payroll tax and employee benefits should also be included.

Other Direct Costs:

Finally, **Other Direct Costs** may be required. Machinery and other equipment may be used also supplies that are directly used in building the product. Each is to be identified and treated accordingly as a part of product cost. During this process, once again the opportunity is there to make adjustments and lower total costs.

Finally, combine Total Material, labor and other costs to arrive at Total Direct Cost. By dividing by the total number of units that have been built in the process, we should arrive at the Total Unit Cost. Having this number, we can use it to calculate our Product Selling Price, as described in Chapter 4.

When marketing of the product begins, a continuing periodic review is highly recommended. Experience will be gained during the selling, purchasing, and/or manufacturing process that will be of great value in locating more adjustments. Always with the goal of improving the Gross Profit, time will be well invested in reviewing actual procedures, costs and expenses. When brisk sales are experienced, for example, delivery terms and timing may be improved to accommodate inventory levels and product availability. Greater quantity discounts may be available, all in the interest of improving profits through Micro-profiting!

c. Rent Expense

It may seem obvious that every company needs a location from which to do business, to sell its products and to store merchandise. But let's take a closer look at the impact of rent on the bottom line, or Net Profit. Let's look at alternatives that might be considered when we need to look for space.

Example 1: Company A is a retail company for which merchandise is purchased and stored until sold over the counter or shipped to mail-order customers. For greater efficiency, merchandise is stored at the same location with over-the-counter sales. The owner decides to rent month to month until the business proves to be stable. The owner rents 2,000 sq. feet at $1.00 per sq. ft. or $2,000 monthly.

Example 2: At the end of year one, the business proves to be successful and a three-year lease is signed at .75 cents per sq. ft., or $1,500 monthly. The lease terms provide for the landlord to provide for the maintenance, saving the tenant approximately $200.00 monthly.

Example 3: At the end of three years, the company exercises an option in the lease to purchase the property for $100,000. Tenant now becomes the property owner, paying zero rent. Payment for the property is made by a down payment of $20,000 and a $80,000 15-year mortgage, payable at $800.00 monthly, of which approximately $350.00 is interest. In addition, the owner will once again pay $200.00 monthly for maintenance.

A summary of the three examples shows:

1. Month-to-month rental was $2,000, or $24,000 annually.
2. Three-year lease was $1,500 monthly and savings of $200 maintenance, or $15,600/ yr.

3. Purchase required $800, including monthly interest of $350. plus $200 maintenance again. or $12,000/ yr.

Property appreciates in value over three years to $175,000, potentially recovering all rent expenses and interest paid over past years if sold.

Another example: Company leases property in a high-value, prestigious area, displaying merchandise at twice the price as in the example above. Result is that rent is high but may raise merchandise to a higher class at higher sales prices, which increases the bottom line.

Another example: Company manufactures inventory in a foreign country at a substantially lower cost. However, shipping costs and tariffs must be added. Owner will be forced to raise prices to maintain a profitable Gross Profit. Volume of merchandise to be sold is a key element in each of the examples above. If, for example, 1,000 units were sold per year, compared with 100,000 units, it would mean that per-unit costs would be greatly changed, as would the net profit.

Giving thought to each of the examples above, there is much to be considered when planning and searching for company space. The planning process must look ahead to inventory size, volume, expected company growth, and available financing to cover the costs and consequences of investing in property. Not to be overlooked in the planning process are the many alternative options in acquiring property and the potential profits from investing in property.

More about rent:

In addition to the basic experiences with rent described above, there are other aspects that could spell the difference between failure or success. One of the most basic factors of being in business is its location. Of course, there is the factor of the best location available to reach intended markets. Imagine the range of locations, from doing business out of one's home to a highly visible and impressive building on 5th Avenue in New York. Is your location required to portray wealth and success to potential buyers, or will it be used primarily for storage?

The point to be made here is that there are many options when selecting a location, along with considerations about how it will be used. Before deciding on the right location, ask yourself these important questions:

1. Will sales be conducted there or will it be used primarily for inventory storage?
2. What is the product size? It will dictate the size of the property needed.
3. Will products be manufactured or assembled or purchased for resale? Again, size will be indicated; also, the outside requirements to provide for deliveries and shipping.

Periodic reviews of present facilities are recommended to assess adequacy, and if expansion will be needed to provide for company growth.

d. Utilities Expense

The expense account of Utilities is one that provides several opportunities for potential reduction. It holds great possibilities for Micro-profiting! While energy generally consists of electricity generated from fossil fuels, the many technologies being developed today from our nations resources create the potential for new alternatives and dramatically lower prices.

Here is a brief summary of the top power sources in the United States, along with their relative availability:

Three major sources are:

- Fossil fuels, that include natural gas and coal
- Nuclear energy
- Renewable energy includes wind, solar, and hydro.

In order of present energy provided in the United States:

Coal	18%
Nuclear power	18%
Wind	10%
Solar	3%
All others	11%
Natural gas	40%

Relative use of these resources varies throughout the US, depending upon availability, such as coal, also to the degree of safety, such as with nuclear power. Wind is rapidly expanding as turbines are being constructed at increasing speed.

My recommendation is for entrepreneurs to be continually aware of energy sources becoming available and the relative costs of each. Cost comparisons will often reveal dramatic differences and opportunities for savings.

In addition to an awareness of alternative energy sources, the creation of company policies for lighting and other uses can lead to additional savings. Policies can include when to turn power off in specific areas and when to avoid using it. Also, where to use gas instead of electricity, and when to use LED power.

The appointment of a specialist within the Company to monitor present usage while watching for improved alternatives can be a powerful assist in the overall improvement of utility expenses.

Finally, by analyzing historical records of energy uses and costs, trends can be identified, and problem areas can be found and remedied. When it comes to Micro-profiting, the area of utilities has much to offer in potential expense savings.

e. Insurance

A current insurance commercial has a great motto: "Only pay for what you need." It is so true, admitting that you need insurance, but not in excess. I believe a careful review of company policies may hold a great opportunity for both improved coverage and savings.

Clearly, we need to insure property owned by the company. That will include real property – buildings and personal property, including furniture, machinery, equipment, and vehicles. It would also include other properties like patents and copyrights. The company also needs liability insurance to cover damage to others. My question would be about how much coverage is needed in each of the categories. In other words, in the event of damage, what will the insurance company pay to replace the losses? This is the area where a professional person, either a trustworthy insurance broker or an appraiser could be of real help to evaluate the properties and assist with placing the right amount of coverage on them. The key is to avoid paying premiums for excess coverage, when realistically, replacement payments in the event of loss would be less.

My recommendation is to locate a knowledgeable insurance broker whom you can trust, and spend time together reviewing and discussing items to be insured. I also recommend comparing the final coverage with the amounts presently in place.

The probability is that a fairly large amount of improvement will be found, that may lower premiums substantially. Micro-profits will strike again in your favor!

f. Salaries & Wages

This account is often one of the largest expense accounts, as it holds payments for all company personnel except those classified as "Direct Labor." The reasons to review Salaries & Wages are contrary to those of other expense accounts, primarily because I do not believe compensation should be reduced for company personnel. As long as individuals are employed, they should be fully paid, along with periodic reviews and upgrades.

If, for good reasons, they are to be terminated, they should be given notice, and termination pay. There should be solid reasons for termination, such as the closing of a department in which they have worked, or completion of a project for which they were hired, or for actions contrary to employment policies.

It is recommended that job descriptions be well understood by both the employee and the reviewer, for evaluation purposes and to assure that work is being performed in accordance with original agreements. A review may also reveal whether certain employee wages should be reclassified as "Direct Labor," which would result in a decrease in "Wages" and an increase in product cost.

Payroll Taxes

Employee taxes are paid to federal and state agencies based on gross wages paid, as described above. No reductions are anticipated in this account unless due to errors in entry and termination.

g. Other Taxes

The largest tax in "Other" is usually property tax, assessed against real property owned by the company. Miscellaneous taxes may also include federal taxes not assessed against payroll, such as excise tax, also state and local taxes. While not always available for reductions, property tax can sometimes be reduced by appeal. An appeal process includes a written application with the state agency, which will be followed by a hearing. A property owner or company officer will have the right to explain reasons for appeal, which may include one or more of the following:

That the property has been rezoned.

Neighborhood downgrades that negatively impact the property.

Damage or deterioration to owner buildings.

When a reasonable presentation is given, supported by evidence, the property owner is frequently granted relief in whole or in part.

By periodically inspecting company owned properties, together with surrounding areas, reasons may be uncovered to file an appeal of taxes. When successful, it can mean a reduction in tax expense in the current year and future periods. It can represent significant savings for the company and a great reduction to be combined with other account adjustments.

h. Phone and Computers

The phone account is no longer the simple account, comprised of the monthly phone bill. In today's world, computers, scanners, and unending varieties of electronic equipment can be found in this category of expense.

A close review of its account may reveal these conditions:

1. That some equipment is large and more appropriately capitalized. It should be reclassified to the balance sheet as "Machinery & Equipment" and depreciated over more than a single year, thereby reducing current expenses.
2. That same equipment is no longer needed amidst the rapidly improving technology. It might be sold or returned for credit.

Because telecommunication is such a new technology, I suggest that over-purchasing of equipment is occasionally possible. Until a complete understanding of the equipment is gained, excess equipment may prove to be unnecessary. It could be returned for credit or resold.

i. Travel & Transportation

Here is an account that may offer the greatest opportunity for savings. It is an account in which large amounts, or should we say, huge amounts are spent to move employees from one location to another. The ways and price levels in which it is accomplished may offer great opportunities for improvement. Or more precisely, expense savings. First, let's look into transportation expenses. It is defined by the IRS as moving from the home place of work of an employee to anywhere within a fifty-mile radius, not requiring overnight lodging.

The many methods of transportation available can be buses, streetcars, taxis, Uber-type vehicles and other public vehicles. Use of these methods might include long-term tickets for frequent users at lower prices, taxis at a higher cost, and other choices, all at different costs.

Company-owned vehicles are possibly the most common means of moving outside the office. The questions here could begin with the make and model of the vehicle to purchase.

Is "impression" high on company priorities? Some companies choose to radiate qualities in all possible ways, including vehicles being used. High quality supports high prices and, thereby, justifies the high-priced vehicles. Other companies support economy cars in just getting the job done. The development of company policies to spell out details of operation, to provide for specific make and model of vehicles for each position in the company is highly important. It not only gives employees direction in their work but controls cost levels in accordance with managerial planning.

A careful review of transportation expenses may reveal opportunities to reduce expenses by selecting slightly lower-cost Consider which position within the company warrants prestigious vehicles, which are mid-priced, and which might drive economy models. A carefully prepared policy could spell out these details, resulting in helpful guidance in purchasing vehicles at considerable savings, leading to all important Micro-profiting! Other provisions of company policy should include the frequency of vehicle maintenance and other steps to ensure a top-condition, dependable fleet.

A close adherence to company policies serves at least two purposes. One is to provide complete records for the IRS, thereby supporting tax deductions claimed. The second is to maintain a level of control over expenses that otherwise could grow out of proportion to company budgets.

Travel:

The extended, longer-term movement from an employee's place of work is termed "travel." It is defined for IRS purposes as requiring overnight lodging, meals, tips and other associated expenses. To fully qualify for tax deductions, the expenses are to be recorded in a contemporaneous log. They are to include purposes, business contacts, activities and amounts paid for each. They must be "ordinary and necessary" and not considered lavish.

Expenses include travel by air, train or vehicle, also taxis, baggage and shipping expenses, lodging, meals, tips, communication, and other related business expenses.

Given the range of expenses included in this category, also the range of associated prices, a careful examination of the Travel Account may reveal excessive amounts and types of expenditures to be disallowed and reduced. These conditions again suggest the importance of company policies in writing. Items included should be the type of air travel, whether first-class economy or charter flights. Also, the level of lodging allowed, whether five-star or less. Possibly the names of hotels should be specified to avoid extravagant use. Also, the business relationship of contacts that will be included in meals and entertainment expenses, the type of ground transportation to use, and business activities described in support of expenses.

This category understandably gives rise to gray areas within the price ranges as well as types of other reasonable expenses. A well-prepared company policy will again be a great assist to employees, guiding them in planning their travel programs and avoiding disallowances of travel reimbursements. It will serve as a strong guide when reviewing the expense account for disallowances and other adjustments.

IRS Publication 463 is highly recommended as a reference for the most current requirements and allowances of transportation and travel expenses.

j. Advertising

Imagine that your promotion and advertising program created such a sensation in the Marketplace that product sales soared and production went full speed to keep up. Profits rose to the sky!

When advertising works, when the word effectively reaches the buying public, sales can happen that are far beyond expectations. The keywords here are "when it works."

A well-prepared program of promotion and advertising can make a world of difference in the potential buyers' responses. Would such a well-prepared program include radio ads, or TV, or a variety of other avenues to the buyer? Appearing on talk shows can be very effective, also the sponsorship of popular community programs like Special Olympics and veterans' programs.

The goal is to reach the greatest number of potential buyers for each dollar spent.

When considering the cost of conventional advertising and the choices available, employing an advertising consultant may be the wisest choice. A good professional should know the cost of each type of media outlet also the best alternate ways in which your product can be promoted at lower costs.

Your product may be so unique and of such great interest and public benefit that it may even make the evening news. Having a deep understanding of one's product, its unique qualities and the demographic audience intended can also be a great help in selecting the best forms of spreading the word.

Some companies believe that "word of mouth" will be the most effective means of advertising over the long term and at the lowest cost. It may be if time is not a large issue. It comes down to knowing your product and the audience you wish to serve. Think of the many sports events and the tens of thousands served at one time with a good game.

Advertising may be a science, but it is also an art to reach your customers in the largest numbers and at the least cost. Devote time in studying the possibilities allowed within your budget, and discuss them with a consultant. Continue your discussions until you feel that your dollars are being spent in the most effective ways. Continue working with the program to improve it, based on your experience and responses.

This may be your largest, most expensive account, the one that can take sales skyward or fall flat. It must be called one of the most important of your expense accounts. Give it your best!

As your program improves, substantial savings may also be the reward, increasing Micro-profits!

k. Repairs and Maintenance

There is a definition that adds relevance to this account. It is something like this: If repairs to company assets add extended life, the costs should be capitalized. In other words, let's say that an old vehicle with excessive mileage is repaired to the extent that it is "as good as new" and should operate for several more years, the repairs should be added to the vehicle's basis. It means that the costs will be removed from Repairs Expenses and capitalized, to be depreciated.

The above is an example of what may be found in the Repairs & Maintenance account.

Expenses can be subjective, but we should be guided by the definition above. As a part of company policies, the treatment of machinery and vehicles should be included in a regularly scheduled maintenance program. It could be scheduled either periodically or on a mileage basis.

The importance of creating a company policy, to include all company fixed assets cannot be overstated. I can say from past experience that the repairs & maintenance account can become a catch-all for expenditures that should be capitalized. A company policy should include steps to be taken regularly to inspect company assets. Over the long term, history has shown that property will operate better, more continually, and at a lower cost.

1. Depreciation Expense

We create most expenses by paying for materials or services to support company activities. Paying for rent and utilities are those kind of expenses. Not so with depreciation. Depreciation begins when we purchase items with an expected useful life of longer than one year. Examples are buildings, vehicles and furniture, with each having an expected useful life exceeding one year. Soap, paper products, and utilities are clearly examples of expenses.

The term for classifying an item as an asset is "capitalizing." It means that it is owned as a property, reported on the Balance Sheet. In instances when an item is small and inexpensive, there can be a question as to whether to classify the item as an asset or as an expense. To clarify this question, many companies have a policy of classifying any purchase over a fixed amount of, say, $500, as an asset. If below that amount it is charged to expense.

Salvage value: This a term used to recognize a lasting value that will remain after depreciation.

For example, a machine is purchased for $20,000, that will last for many years. While it is assigned a useful life to depreciate of ten years, it will still remain in good useful condition following the depreciation period. When purchased, it is assigned an estimated salvage value of, say $2,000, with the remaining $18,000 to be depreciated.

There are two basic methods of depreciation, although a few more are sometimes used. The first, and most common, is a straight line. When using this method, the cost is simply divided by the estimated useful life. If, for example, the life selected is ten years, then one-tenth, or 10% will be depreciated, or charged to expense annually.

The second method is referred to as "accelerated" or faster depreciation. It is approved by the IRS when tax reporting. Using the example above of a $20,000 machine purchase, the same 10% rate is determined as one-tenth of the cost. However, for this method, the 10% is doubled to 20%, and applied to the remaining undepreciated balance each year. An example would be Year 1: $20,000 cost less (20,000 x .20) or $4,000. Year 2 would be: $20,000 less $4,000, or $16,000 undepreciated less (16,000 x .20) or $3,200. Year 3 would be $20,000 Less $4,000, less 3,200 = $12,800 undepreciated less (12,800 less 2,560) = 10,240. It will charge the same amount to expense over its life, but at a faster rate in the early years.

Note that while a straight line would be used for accounting purposes and when preparing the balance sheet, the accelerated or double-declining balance method could be used for tax purposes to create more deductible expenses and reduce taxable income.

Calculations should be reviewed at least monthly for correct application. Permanent worksheets should be prepared to calculate depreciation and retain them, to be included when preparing tax returns. Depreciation is properly reported on the Balance Sheet as a reduction of asset cost, shown as follows:

Machinery & equipment $50,000

Less Allowance for depreciation $12,000

Book Value $38,000

As noted, the term for depreciated assets is Book Value. The asset no longer holds the original cost but is properly reported as shown above. In the event of a sale, gain or loss would be calculated by selling price less book value.

m. Other Expenses

Most companies have at least one or two unique expenditures during the year, slightly less than typical. The question is where to classify them? Our listing of expenses in Chapter 4 does not include Legal expenses, Supplies or Computer expenses.

If an expenditure does not seem to have a logical account to which it can be assigned, just place it in "Other" and describe it slightly. The accountant will give special attention to this. A new account might be opened for it, or It may remain in "Other and given an explanation. Every expenditure should have a purpose, even if it is classified as "Other."

9

The Micro-Profits Committee

Achieving incremental improvements is essential to long-term success in the fast-paced world of business. We go into greater detail on the need for methodical techniques in this chapter in order to realize the potential for micro-profits. Businesses can increase their profitability and advance toward greater wealth by concentrating on small, incremental increases.

Highlighting the Necessity of Methodical Approaches

Understanding the value of methodical techniques is crucial as we work to maximize profitability. Businesses need to implement structured procedures that enable continuous improvement over time instead of depending just on intermittent efforts or one-time fixes. Businesses can establish a framework for locating, evaluating, and seizing chances for incremental improvements by putting systematic methods into practice.

This strategic team is committed to leading efforts to discover and implement micro-profit strategies across many sectors of the business. We establish the notion of "The Micro-Profits Committee" to institutionalize the pursuit of micro-profits within an organization. The committee is the driving force behind the company's pursuit of incremental gains; it is made up of individuals with a variety of experience and a common commitment to maximizing profitability.

The Committee for Micro-Profits' Role

Functioning as a committed task force, the Micro-Profits Committee is tasked with scrutinizing every facet of the enterprise to identify prospects for enhancement. The committee finds areas where minor changes can have a big impact through group brainstorming sessions, data-driven analysis, and strategic planning.

1. Undertaking Extensive Evaluations: In order to identify areas with unrealized potential for micro profits, the committee thoroughly evaluates the business's operations, finances, marketing plans, and other areas.
2. Creating Tailored Strategies: In light of its conclusions, the committee creates customized plans meant to capture small profits in particular company domains. Efficiency, cutting expenses, increasing revenue, and total profitability are given top priority in these tactics.
3. Putting Actionable Solutions into Practice: The committee puts specific, goal-oriented solutions into practice that are intended to produce observable outcomes. Every endeavor is meticulously planned and carried out, whether it involves finding new revenue streams, optimizing resources, or simplifying operations.
4. Tracking and Assessing Progress: The Micro-Profits Committee keeps tabs on the results of strategies put into action, keeping tabs on key performance metrics and calculating the effect on the business's bottom line. They make sure that activities are still in line with the major business goals by regularly assessing their success.

Extending The Micro-Profits Committee's Function

The Micro-Profits Committee's influence is further amplified by creating specialized sub-teams to handle certain areas of potential, in addition to its primary duty of devising and executing micro-profit plans. Recognizing the critical role that diverse income streams play in optimizing profitability, one such sub-team is devoted to investigating new sales possibilities.

The Micro-Profits Committee creates a special sub-team tasked with investigating cutting-edge sales opportunities because they recognize the value of expanding into new markets and revenue streams. Those with experience in business development, strategic planning, and market research make up this sub-team, which is responsible for finding unexplored avenues for revenue growth outside of conventional sales channels.

Members from all areas of the organization participate in cooperative brainstorming sessions led by The Micro-Profits Committee to initiate the exploration process. The purpose of these meetings is to provide ideas, stimulate creativity, and pinpoint possible sales channels that complement the company's distinct advantages and competitive positioning.

After conducting thorough research and deliberation, the committee determines several viable sales channels that are appropriate for the particular characteristics of the enterprise. Direct sales to customers, online stores, joint ventures, affiliate marketing plans, and more could be among them.

The Micro-Profits Committee establishes a special subcommittee with the responsibility of forming alliances with corresponding companies and organizations because it recognizes the potential of strategic partnerships to increase market reach and spur revenue growth. In order to find possible partners, negotiate advantageous agreements, and support cooperative initiatives, this subcommittee makes use of the experience of cross-functional team members.

The Sales Avenues Exploration Sub-Team's principal duties include

1. Market Analysis and Research: The sub-team carries out in-depth market analysis to pinpoint new trends, customer inclinations, and growth prospects. They can obtain important insights into possible sales channels by examining competition strategy and market data.
2. Planning and Execution of Strategic Plans: The sub-team creates plans that specify how to go about investigating and utilizing new sales channels in light of the study findings. They manage the execution of projects, set precise goals, and distribute resources wisely.
3. Testing and Pilot Programs: The sub-team may start testing or pilot programs to reduce risks and confirm the viability of new sales channels. They improve their strategy and increase the likelihood of success by getting input, calculating performance indicators, and making necessary adjustments to tactics.
4. Close cooperation between the Sales Avenues Exploration Sub-Team and the Strategic Partnerships Sub-Committee is maintained in order to investigate potential joint ventures, distribution contracts, co-marketing campaigns, and other cooperative projects that promote mutual growth.

Businesses can boost revenue production and achieve long-term, sustainable success in the marketplace by proactively identifying and utilizing new sales outlets through the coordinated efforts of The Micro-Profits Committee and its specialist sub-teams.

Establishing an Expert After-Sales Services Group

Continuing its tradition of all-encompassing quality, The Micro-Profits Committee launches the creation of a dedicated staff for post-purchase services. This team is made up of people with experience in process optimization, customer relationship management, and service delivery. Their job is to come up with and put into action plans that will improve the experience that customers have after making a purchase.

The Micro-Profits Committee facilitates brainstorming sessions to find successful after-sales tactics that have the biggest impact without requiring a sizable financial commitment. The committee does this because it recognizes the need to maximize resources and reduce financial inputs. These brainstorming meetings bring together cross-functional teams to discuss ideas, best practices, and novel after-sale service delivery strategies.

The following are the team's primary areas of focus

1. Enhancing customer interaction and support tools to rapidly resolve post-purchase issues, problems, and feedback is the emphasis of the dedicated team. They guarantee prompt responses and individualized client service by utilizing technology and automation when applicable.
2. Value-Added Services and Upselling Possibilities: The group looks for ways to provide value-added services and upsell possibilities to customers that go beyond meeting their immediate needs and enhance their initial purchase. This could include special offers catered to the interests of certain customers, maintenance plans, supplementary goods, and extended warranties.
3. Proactively Resolving Issues and Developing Relationships: The after-sales services staff shows a dedication to relationship development and customer satisfaction by proactively recognizing and resolving possible problems or pain points encountered by clients. Proactively communicating and

resolving issues cultivate trust and loyalty, converting contented clients into brand ambassadors.

4. Constant Improvement and Integration of Customer Feedback: The specialist team establishes a culture of constant improvement by routinely analyzing post-purchase procedures and asking clients for input to pinpoint areas that could be improved. They guarantee continued relevance and efficacy by adjusting their tactics and service offerings in response to real-time input.

Examining Effective Cases in Distribution Channel Diversification

Diversifying distribution channels is crucial for achieving sustainable economic growth, as demonstrated by an analysis of the tactics used by successful businesses like Walt Disney and General Mills. These businesses are excellent illustrations of how pursuing sales opportunities beyond a single product may result in substantial growth and a wider reach into the market.

Example Case Study: General Mills

The international food giant General Mills has effectively broadened its distribution network to spur expansion and increase its market share worldwide. With a diversified portfolio that includes over 100 well-known brands and products that are distributed in 170 countries worldwide, the company has become a leader in the food sector thanks to its strategic approach to diversification.

Expansion of Product Portfolio: General Mills saw the value of adding more products to its lineup outside of its core offers. The company has grown into a number of categories, including breakfast cereals, snacks, baking items, and more, through partnerships, strategic acquisitions, and product innovation. General Mills has been able to expand its customer base and gain market share in a number of different categories because of this diversity.

International Market Penetration: To take advantage of worldwide demand, General Mills has concentrated on entering foreign markets in addition to broadening its product line. The company has taken use of its diverse distribution channels to expand its customer base and boost sales outside of its home market by forging a strong global presence in strategic locations.

Channel Optimization: General Mills has embraced a multichannel distribution approach, combining e-commerce sites, direct-to-consumer programs, and conventional retail channels. The company has improved accessibility to its products and strengthened its competitive position in the market by streamlining its distribution methods to satisfy changing consumer demands.

Outcomes and Implications

General Mills has seen notable commercial success and economic growth as a result of its strategic approach to distribution channel diversification. Because of its diverse product line and global reach, the company has been able to weather market ups and downs, reduce the risks associated with relying too much on a single product, and seize new growth opportunities. General Mills leads innovation in the food sector and provides value to stakeholders globally by consistently pursuing new sales opportunities and adjusting to shifting consumer tastes.

The General Mills case study demonstrates how strategically diversified distribution channels can significantly boost market competitiveness and economic growth. Businesses may open up new revenue streams, broaden their market reach, and achieve long-term, sustainable success in an increasingly changing business environment by adopting General Mills' strategy and utilizing a variety of distribution channels.

Walt Disney Case Study: Extending Beyond Animation

A great example of a business that cleverly expanded its distribution channels to achieve impressive economic growth is Walt Disney, which is well-known for its famous characters, such as Mickey and Minnie Mouse. Disney has come a long way from its modest animation roots to offer a diverse array of entertainment options, such as feature films, television networks, and theme parks.

Walt Disney firm's transition into Full-Length Films: Although it was first known for its animated short films with Mickey and Minnie Mouse, the firm realized full-length feature films could capture the attention of people on a bigger scale. Disney showcased its storytelling and animation prowess through the creation of enduring cinematic experiences with iconic films like "Cinderella" and "Snow White and the Seven Dwarfs."

The Development of Theme Parks: Disney's entry into the theme park sector represented a major expansion of its lines of distribution. The firm created immersive entertainment locations that allowed visitors to feel the enchantment of Disney directly with the launch of Disneyland in 1955 and Walt Disney World Resort in 1971. Along with bringing in a sizable sum of money, the popularity of these theme parks strengthened Disney's brand recognition and encouraged patronage.

Disney extended its reach by acquiring ESPN and ABC Broadcasting in 1996. Disney did this after realizing the potential of television as a distribution medium. Through ABC's network of television channels, this calculated move gave Disney access to a large audience, enabling the business to show off its material to audiences across the country. Disney further cemented its position in the media landscape by acquiring ESPN in 1996, which allowed it to take advantage of the increasing demand for digital content and sports programming.

Outcomes and Implications:

Walt Disney achieved previously unheard-of levels of economic growth and market supremacy because of the diversity of its distribution channels. Disney became a worldwide entertainment superpower by diversifying its revenue streams and going beyond animation into industries like full-length films, theme parks, and media networks. In an industry that is always changing, the company has been able to stay relevant and profitable by embracing new technologies and adapting to changing consumer tastes. The transformational effect of purposeful distribution channel diversification is exemplified by Walt Disney's rise from a modest animation studio to a multidimensional entertainment giant. Disney has developed a massive ecosystem of entertainment experiences that never ceases to enthrall audiences of all ages worldwide by utilizing its renowned brands and storytelling prowess across a variety of channels.

Long-Term Planning and Management

The foundational elements of long-term planning and efficient management support the steady expansion and prosperity of businesses in all sectors. Walt Disney and General Mills are two companies that highlight the value of strong leadership and strategic vision in establishing long-term success in challenging business environments.

General Mills: Growth through Strategic Reinvestment

Strategically reinvested profits fuel development and innovation, demonstrating General Mills' dedication to long-term planning and management. In order to be competitive in the ever-evolving food business, the company's leadership understands how important it is to continuously innovate its product portfolio, increase its global footprint, and optimize its operations. General Mills reinvests its profits into R&D projects, product diversification, and market expansion endeavors through wise financial management and intelligent resource allocation. The organization maintains its relevance and resonates with customers globally by keeping a close eye on rising trends and changing consumer preferences.

Walt Disney: Creative Development and Brand Establishment

Walt Disney's long-term vision and sound management techniques are also credited with the company's continued success; these factors helped it grow from a modest animation studio to a major global entertainment empire. Disney's executives have proven to have a deep awareness of the ways in which storytelling, originality, and brand development can captivate the hearts and minds of people everywhere. Disney's commitment to providing unmatched entertainment experiences has inspired its long-term planning, from the birth of iconic characters like Mickey Mouse to the expansion into full-length movies and the construction of theme parks worldwide. Disney continues to attract audiences across generations by utilizing its rich tradition of narrative and invention. It also diversifies its revenue streams through well-timed investments and acquisitions.

Principal Learnings

The importance of long-term planning is shown by Walt Disney and General Mills, who see it as a vital part of their expansion plans. These businesses provide the foundation for long-term success by defining clear objectives, seeing emerging trends, and making calculated investments. Steadying long-term growth and overcoming obstacles are mostly dependent on competent management and leadership. The leadership teams at Walt Disney and General Mills are able to guide their businesses toward prolonged success because they possess vision, flexibility, and a proactive approach to decision-making. Both businesses understand the value of strategically allocating their revenues to new product development, market expansion, and innovative ideas. Walt Disney and General Mills are at the forefront of their respective sectors because they never stop innovating and looking for new ways to develop.

Thus, effective management and long-term planning are critical components of Walt Disney and General Mills' continued success. With their long legacies and success stories, these organizations inspire others and prosper in a constantly changing business world by embracing innovation, promoting creativity, and adhering to their basic beliefs.

Growth-Catalysts

Proactive and strategic action is essential for long-term growth and success in the ever-changing business market. To take advantage of possibilities and lessen obstacles, businesses must constantly innovate, assess their strengths and shortcomings, and implement corrective actions. Examples of companies that embrace ongoing innovation and action to advance their growth agendas are General Mills and Walt Disney.

Strengths and Weaknesses:

Companies should thoroughly evaluate their strengths and limitations before launching any growth activities so that their strategic choices are well-informed. This entails assessing competitive advantages, market positioning, and internal capabilities to pinpoint areas in need of development and growth prospects.:

Implementing Remedial Measures:

After identifying their strengths and limitations, businesses need to fix their shortcomings and build on their strengths. This could entail making investments in infrastructural improvements, hiring new employees, or rearranging corporate plans to better suit consumer needs and new trends.

Instances of Strategic and Optimistic Behavior:

1. Extending Markets: To support their respective growth paths, General Mills and Walt Disney have both adopted aggressive market expansion strategies. Growing markets offer chances for more revenue and market share, whether via overseas expansion or market penetration into new demographics.
2. Creating complimentary Products: Businesses can make use of their current assets and capabilities to create products or services that are complimentary and meet changing consumer demands. Businesses can maximize consumer loyalty and expand into new

market sectors by providing a wide array of products that supplement their primary offers.

3. Undertaking Extensive Research on Sales Demographics: Product development and marketing strategies that are successful depend on having a thorough understanding of the preferences and demographics of the target market. Through comprehensive research on sales demographics, businesses can acquire a significant understanding of customer behavior, buying habits, and industry developments. This allows them to customize their marketing approaches and product offerings appropriately.

The key to promoting growth and attaining sustained success is to adopt proactive and strategic measures, including broadening markets, creating supplementary goods, and carrying out in-depth analyses of sales demographics. Businesses should position themselves for competitiveness and sustained success in today's changing business environment by adopting innovation, agility, and a proactive approach.

Micro-Strategizing for Achievement: Managing the Way to Extended Expansion

To achieve sustained success, ongoing micro-planning becomes essential for maintaining the trajectory of broad objectives and guaranteeing flexibility in response to changing market conditions. In order to negotiate the challenges of today's business world and promote sustainable growth, successful firms understand the value of agility, creativity, and well-informed decision-making.

Ongoing strategy and technique evaluation, modification, and improvement at the granular level in order to bring them into line with more general organizational goals is known as continuous micro-planning. To remain adaptable to shifting market conditions and new prospects, it comprises dividing up long-term plans into manageable steps, keeping an eye on the situation, and making appropriate modifications.

Successful organizations exhibit agility and resilience in a dynamic marketplace by promptly adjusting to changes in consumer preferences, competitive environments, and technology breakthroughs. By means of ongoing micro-planning, organizations can proactively detect developing patterns, foresee changes in the market, and modify their approaches correspondingly to sustain their significance and competitive edge.

In order to increase productivity, maximize resources, and open up new revenue streams, micro-planning also entails investigating cutting-edge methods for operations, procedures, and business models. Companies that cultivate a culture of experimentation and creativity are better able to streamline processes, find new ways to operate and seize growth possibilities.

Effective micro-planning is centered on making well-informed decisions. Businesses use data-driven insights and customer feedback to inform resource allocation and investment decisions. Companies can find opportunities, prioritize investments, and maximize returns on investment by thoroughly researching and analyzing customer behavior, market trends, and competitive landscapes.

Patience for Development: Fostering Achievement via Long-Term Planning

Since long-term planning takes time to actualize, achieving sustainable growth requires patience. Taking after successful models requires a strong commitment to steady, patient work, as well as a commitment to constructive behavior and ongoing development. Businesses are better equipped to handle obstacles, seize opportunities, and accomplish their long-term goals when they recognize the need for patience in the growth process.

As a road map for accomplishing organizational goals over a prolonged period of time, long-term planning is the cornerstone of sustainable growth. However, the results of strategic investments and efforts frequently take time to materialize because the choices we make today might not have an impact on our lives for some time. Hence, patience is crucial since it enables businesses to maintain focus on their long-term goals and endure despite inescapable obstacles and disappointments along the route.

Learning from the experiences of successful industry leaders requires perseverance. Sustainable growth is founded on a foundation of patience and regular efforts, despite the temptation to seek quick fixes or shortcuts. Organizations can learn a great deal about the value of patience, endurance, and a strong commitment to constructive actions by examining the tactics and procedures of prosperous businesses.

Realizing growth goals over time requires a dedication to constructive behavior and ongoing development. This means being proactive in addressing obstacles and grabbing opportunities, as well as creating and executing sensible strategies and goals. Through the promotion of an innovative, cooperative, and flexible culture, businesses can successfully secure sustained success.

10

Building Customer Relationships

In today's dynamic and competitive business environment, maximizing revenue and profitability is a top priority for businesses across industries. One effective approach to achieving this goal is by implementing strategies to increase transaction value. By focusing on enhancing the average transaction value, creating bundled offers, and upselling complementary products, businesses can capitalize on each customer interaction to drive incremental revenue and strengthen customer relationships. We will explore these strategies in detail and highlight their significance in driving business growth and success. For businesses to keep a base of devoted clients, encourage recurring business, and cultivate enduring connections, they must implement effective customer retention methods.

Individualized Communication: Businesses can engage with customers more deeply by setting up channels for individualized communication. This can involve sending out customized emails, messages, or offers based on a person's preferences and past purchases.

Rewards and Loyalty Programs: Putting reward and loyalty programs in place encourages clients to keep making purchases from the company. Rewarding customers with discounts, special offers, or freebies in response to their volume or frequency of purchases promotes repeat business.

Outstanding Customer Service: Maintaining a customer base is greatly aided by offering outstanding customer service. Immediate attention to complaints, efficient problem-solving, and a satisfying experience in general can convert unhappy consumers into devoted brand ambassadors.

Consistent Engagement: Keeping the brand at the forefront of consumers' minds requires continuing to communicate with them consistently via a variety of platforms, including blogs, newsletters, and social media. Providing clients with updates, promotions, and relevant information keeps them interested in the company and engaged.

High-quality Goods and Services: Relentlessly providing goods or services of the highest caliber fosters brand confidence and trust. If customers think the company's offerings are valuable, they are more likely to stick around.

Exclusive Offers and Sneak Peaks: Giving current customers access to limited-edition items, exclusive offers, or sneak peaks of upcoming products helps them feel important and valued. This exclusivity can help people feel more connected to the company.

Community Building: Fostering a feeling of community among clients via social media groups, online discussion boards, or in-person gatherings promotes engagement and allegiance. Consumers are more inclined to stick with a company if they feel like they are part of a community.

Surprise and Delight: Giving consumers something unexpected, like free samples, birthday discounts, or handwritten thank-you notes, can make an impression on them and improve their emotional bond with the business.

Continuous Improvement: To keep the business current and responsive to the needs of its clients, it is important to continuously analyze data, monitor customer feedback, and adjust tactics in response to shifting trends and preferences.

As these pointers are mentioned on their very base level, it is necessary to know that it takes more, a lot more, to get the business where it should be. For businesses looking to achieve long-term success and consistent growth, effective client retention techniques are essential. Building enduring relationships with clients is essential to these tactics. Businesses should put more effort into developing trust and emotional ties than just making sales. Fostering loyalty and promoting repeat business requires constantly exceeding expectations at every engagement and placing a high priority on client pleasure. By using customer relationship management (CRM) systems, companies may keep track of consumer interactions, preferences, and feedback, which makes future encounters more efficient and customized.

Loyalty Programs

By providing rewards for ongoing business, loyalty programs are crucial in keeping clients. These initiatives show gratitude and persuade consumers to pick the brand over rivals. Examples of these initiatives include point-based systems, tiered rewards, and special benefits for devoted consumers. Personalized client interaction is yet another essential component of successful retention campaigns. Businesses are able to customize offers, and recommendations, and communicate to each consumer based on their unique interests and habits by utilizing customer data. Whether via product recommendations, tailored mailings, or exclusive promos, this individualized approach upholds the brand's value and fortifies consumer relationships.

Communication and Support

Continual support and communication are necessary to keep customers. To guarantee a great customer experience all the way through the customer journey, businesses should be proactive in responding to questions, issues, and feedback from customers. Customers are engaged and connected to the brand when they receive regular updates on new items, promotions, or pertinent information. Furthermore, proactively obtaining and addressing client feedback indicates a dedication to ongoing enhancement. Businesses can learn about the requirements and preferences of their customers by often asking for feedback via surveys, reviews, or direct communication channels. By making adjustments in response to this criticism, the company shows that it respects client opinions and is committed to providing a first-rate service. The key components of successful customer retention strategies include individualized customer interaction, loyalty program implementation, and long-term relationship cultivation. Businesses can increase client loyalty, encourage repeat business, and eventually see sustainable profits over time by giving these factors top priority.

CRM

Actively listening to customer input and using it to drive significant improvements that benefit the company and its clients are key components of developing good customer relationships. Businesses show that they are receptive to client requirements and increase their bottom line by turning suggestions from customers into improvements that generate profits.

First and foremost, companies need to set up efficient systems for gathering and evaluating client feedback. These could be questionnaires, feedback forms, social media tracking, or direct lines of contact. Businesses can show their customers that they value and consider their thoughts by actively seeking feedback from them. After feedback has been received, it is critical to thoroughly examine it in order to pinpoint recurring themes, problems, and opportunities for development. Making decisions is aided by the useful insights this study offers on the tastes and expectations of customers.

Next, companies have to rank and put into practice practical recommendations that could increase revenue. This could entail improving already-existing goods or services, optimizing workflows for increased effectiveness, or launching brand-new items in response to market demand. Businesses increase their competitive advantage and improve the customer experience by taking client comments into consideration. Brands that show a dedication to paying attention to and meeting the demands of their customers are more likely to win over new customers over time.

Additionally, companies can use customer reviews as a marketing tool to draw in new clients and hold onto current ones. Emphasizing enhancements made in response to feedback from customers conveys openness and a commitment to ongoing development, which builds loyalty and trust. Businesses can also make money off of consumer input by creating upgraded or premium versions of their goods or services according to what customers want. These value-added products have the potential to bring in more money and attract higher prices.

All things considered, turning consumer feedback into revenue-generating enhancements is a win-win approach for companies and clients. Businesses may boost profitability, preserve a competitive edge in the market, and build stronger relationships by actively seeking out customer input and making effective adjustments.

New Era

In the current digital era, businesses have access to a wide range of online platforms and technologies that help them collect insightful client data. In order to promote educated decision-making and raise overall customer happiness, these platforms are essential for gathering, evaluating, and interpreting consumer input. The following are some of the most important websites and resources for obtaining insightful data:

Survey Tools: Companies can design personalized surveys to get client feedback by using platforms such as SurveyMonkey, Google Forms, or Typeform. These surveys can be used to gather information on many facets of the customer experience and can be delivered by email, social media, or website embedding.

Social Media Monitoring Tools: Businesses can track and examine discussions and mentions on various social media sites by utilizing tools like Hootsuite, Sprout Social, or Buffer. Businesses can obtain important insights into the sentiment, preferences, and trends of their customers by monitoring hashtags, keywords, and brand mentions.

Online review platforms: Reviews and ratings from users on websites such as Yelp, Google Reviews, and TripAdvisor offer insightful user feedback. Companies are able to address customer issues, highlight positive experiences, and pinpoint areas for improvement by keeping an eye on and responding to reviews on these platforms.

Tools for website analytics: Sites like Hotjar and Google Analytics provide data on user activity, traffic, and navigation. Through the examination of data like bounce rate, session length, and click-through rates, companies may enhance the user experience of their websites by optimizing their design and content.

Platforms for managing feedback: Applications such as Medallia, Qualtrics, or Zendesk collect input from social media, support tickets, surveys, and other channels, centralizing it into insights that may be put to use. These platforms promote continuous development by assisting companies in effectively prioritizing and addressing client input.

User testing platforms: Companies can test usability and get input from actual users by using platforms like UserTesting or UserZoom. Businesses can pinpoint usability problems, pain points, and areas for improvement by watching how consumers engage with products or prototypes. Businesses can gain important insights into the tastes, actions, and expectations of their customers by utilizing these internet platforms and technologies. Strategic decision-making, product innovation, and, ultimately the whole consumer experience are all influenced by these findings.

Maximize Income and Profitability

To maximize income and profitability, initiatives to boost transaction value must be put into practice. Here are some more tactics that emphasize raising average transaction value, taking advantage of bundled offers, and upselling related products:

1. Methods to Increase Average Transaction Value:

- Cross-selling: Make recommendations for customers on similar or complimentary products in light of their recent purchases. Offer recommendations for add-ons like lenses or memory cards, for instance, if a customer purchases a camera.
- Value-added services: Provide extras or improvements to customers' purchases to make them better. Extended warranties, installation assistance, and customization choices are a few examples of this.
- Volume discounts: Provide discounts to consumers who make greater purchases in order to entice them to do so. This tactic encourages buyers to stock up on goods while also raising the transaction value.
- Time-limited promotions: Build suspense by providing special discounts or promos that are only available for a short while. Customers are encouraged to make further purchases during their current visit with limited-time discounts.

2. Building Packaged Deals:

- Group related things together and sell them for less than you would pay if you bought them separately. A technology merchant might, for instance, include a mouse, antivirus software, and a traveling case with a laptop.
- Emphasize to customers the value proposition of bundled offerings by stressing the convenience and cost benefits of buying many things at once.
- To ensure relevancy and attractiveness, customize bundles depending on consumer preferences or past purchases.

3. Promoting Supplementary Items:

- Upselling is convincing potential clients to upgrade to a more expensive or upscale version of the product they are thinking about. Giving a bigger size or a high-end model with more features, for instance.
- Highlight the advantages and value-added of the upsell, such as increased functionality, better performance, or increased durability.
- Employ suggestive selling strategies and creative product placement to highlight upsell chances to customers while they are making a purchase.

Firms seeking to optimize income and profitability must put into practice ways to raise transaction value through tactics including raising the average transaction value, developing bundled offers, and upselling complementary items. By concentrating on these tactics, companies can boost revenue while simultaneously offering customers additional value, which promotes customer happiness and loyalty. Maintaining competitiveness and prospering in the market will depend on how well these strategies are adjusted and optimized as the business environment changes further.

11

Optimizing Operational Expenses

Reducing operating expenses is a key tactic for long-term success in the quest for productivity and earnings. An essential component of this optimization process is putting in place effective cost-cutting procedures. Through the identification of inefficient areas and the implementation of focused steps to optimize processes, companies can attain substantial cost reductions while maintaining optimal performance and quality. In this chapter, we'll examine the significance of developing a productive procedure for cutting costs as well as useful strategies for efficiently managing and minimizing operating expenses.

Realizing the wide variety of industries in which your company may operate, we encourage reading all of the material in this chapter, after which you will be in the best position to focus on the areas that apply to your company.

An extensive evaluation of present operations is necessary to pinpoint areas where expenses can be reduced or eliminated before establishing an effective method for cost reduction can be established. This includes examining a number of business-related factors, such as supply chain management, manufacturing procedures, overhead costs, and resource usage. Businesses can identify inefficiencies, redundancies, and inefficient practices that add to excessive expenditures by carrying out a thorough analysis.

Following the identification of improvement areas, companies can launch focused cost-cutting programs that are adapted to their unique requirements and situations. This could include looking for other vendors with competitive pricing or renegotiating contracts with suppliers to obtain better terms. Optimizing inventory management procedures can also lower the danger of having too many or obsolete goods and cut carrying expenses. Long-term labor expenses can be decreased, productivity can be raised, and operations can be streamlined by investing in automation and technology. Accounting, customer relationship management (CRM), and inventory management software solutions can be implemented to optimize workflows, boost accuracy, and do away with manual labor, freeing up staff to concentrate on value-added duties.

Businesses should look into ways to cut costs through waste reduction programs, energy efficiency initiatives, and sustainable practices in addition to tackling operational inefficiencies. Businesses that adopt eco-friendly methods not only cut expenses but also improve their brand recognition and attract customers who care about the environment. Furthermore, cultivating a culture of cost awareness and responsibility among staff members is crucial for long-term cost reduction initiatives. Employers can foster a culture of accountability and promote ongoing development across the board by giving staff members the freedom to find cost-saving measures and encouraging them to own the procedure.

All things considered, developing an effective strategy for cutting costs necessitates a methodical approach, careful analysis, and proactive management. In today's competitive business environment, firms can position themselves for long-term success, create considerable savings, and increase competitiveness by prioritizing cost-reduction projects and utilizing technology, innovation, and employee engagement.

Optimizing operational efficiency and cutting expenses efficiently requires the use of optimized processes. Here's how companies can reduce costs by implementing efficient processes:

Process Mapping and Analysis

To find inefficiencies, start by mapping out the current processes. Examine every stage of the procedure to identify areas where resources and time are being wasted. This may be related to getting employee input.

Standardization and Simplification

Whenever feasible, standardize and streamline procedures after inefficiencies have been found. Simplifying operations by getting rid of pointless stages, combining related work together, and creating explicit policies and norms can save money and boost output dramatically. To encourage uniformity and effectiveness across the entire company, concentrate on standardizing procedures amongst teams and departments.

Automation and Technology Integration

Use automation and technological tools to reduce labor-intensive or repetitive operations. By using software for document management, data input, and workflow automation, businesses may decrease human error, speed up processing, and give staff members more time to work on higher-value tasks. Seek chances to reduce data clusters and enhance departmental collaboration by streamlining data flow and integrating systems.

Resource Optimization

Match resources to demand more effectively to maximize resource allocation. In order to reduce the expenses associated with retaining excess inventory by putting in place just-in-time inventory management systems or employing predictive analytics to estimate demand and modify production schedules accordingly. To cut expenses related to hiring full-time staff, think about outsourcing non-core operations or using independent contractors and freelancers for specialized work.

Continuous Improvement

Foster a culture of continuous improvement by routinely

encouraging staff members to find and recommend process enhancements. Putting in place a structured feedback system, such as suggestion boxes, recurring team meetings, or online idea-sharing platforms, can help uncover areas for cost savings and promote continuous process improvement.

Training and Development

Make investments in the education and training of your staff members to guarantee that they possess the abilities and know-how required to carry out efficient procedures. Train staff members on new technology, process enhancements, and best practices to enable them to support cost-cutting initiatives and boost organizational effectiveness. Businesses can lower expenses, increase operational effectiveness, and boost their competitiveness in the market by putting in place streamlined processes. Businesses may sustain cost reduction efforts over time and set themselves up for long-term success by consistently reviewing and optimizing processes.

Set Business Examples

Production System for Toyota:

TPS is the number of transactions handled or finished in a second in the context of computing or systems. It's an essential indicator for evaluating the effectiveness and performance of systems, especially in settings like financial, online retail, or database management systems where there are a lot of transactions. TPS monitoring aids in assessing system capacity, locating performance bottlenecks, and guaranteeing that the system can manage the workload efficiently without sacrificing dependability or speed.

JIT is a management concept and approach designed to increase productivity and decrease waste in manufacturing operations. Although it was first used in the industrial sector, it is now used in many other industries. The fundamental principle of Just-In-Time (JIT) manufacturing involves producing and delivering items or services exactly when customers need them rather than accumulating surplus inventory or maintaining huge inventories of raw materials, work-in-progress, or finished goods.

The Japanese word "kaizen" means "continuous improvement." It's a way of thinking and working that emphasizes constant, small-scale improvements to systems, services, goods, and processes. Among the fundamental tenets of Kaizen are:

Respect for people: Encouraging and enabling staff members at all levels to offer suggestions and take part in initiatives for change. Gemba, which means "where value is created," places a strong emphasis on the observation and in-depth examination of work processes in order to spot areas that could use improvement. Standardization: Creating policies and practices to serve as a foundation for ongoing efforts to improve. Muda, or the elimination of waste, is the process of determining which resources, activities, or processes contribute no value to the final good or service.

Toyota's well-known TPS is a shining example of effective manufacturing cost optimization. TPS incorporates concepts like Just-In-Time (JIT) inventory management and continuous improvement (Kaizen) to maximize productivity, reduce waste, and increase efficiency. By lowering the cost of carrying inventory, cutting down on production waste, and improving overall operational efficiency, Toyota has implemented TPS and saved a significant amount of money. Toyota has been able to continue making profitable cars at competitive pricing thanks to this.

Fulfillment Centers for Amazon:

Amazon's fulfillment centers are prime examples of effective supply chain management and logistics cost minimization. Amazon uses data analytics, robotics, and cutting-edge technology to increase warehouse productivity, lower shipping costs, and streamline operations. Amazon reduces labor costs, maximizes warehouse space usage, and optimizes shipping routes using automation, optimization algorithms, and real-time data analysis. This leads to quicker order fulfillment and cheaper operational expenses.

The Efficiency of Walmart's Supply Chain:

Walmart is well-known for its effective supply chain management techniques, which allow the retail behemoth to continue being profitable while continuing to provide customers with cheap pricing. Walmart uses strategies like cross-docking, vendor-managed inventory (VMI), and effective logistics for transportation to streamline its supply chain. Walmart lowers costs across the whole supply chain, from sourcing to delivery, by collaborating closely with suppliers, managing inventory levels, and taking advantage of economies of scale. This eventually translates into reduced prices for customers and enhanced competition in the retail market.

Cloud-Based Infrastructure of Netflix:

Netflix's move to a cloud-based infrastructure serves as an excellent illustration of how to successfully optimize costs in the technology industry. Netflix has eliminated the need for expensive on-premises hardware, software licenses, and maintenance by moving its IT infrastructure to the cloud. Moving an IT infrastructure usually relates to transferring all the digital tools and systems a company uses to store, process, and manage data and information from one location to another. This could involve physical equipment like servers and networking devices, as well as virtual assets like software applications and databases. It's like relocating the nerve center of a company's digital operations from one place to another, which requires careful planning and execution to ensure minimal disruption to the business.

With this change, Netflix is able to focus on providing customers with premium streaming services at a reasonable price, scale its operations more effectively, and save infrastructure expenditures. Furthermore, the flexibility and agility of cloud-based infrastructure allow Netflix to quickly adjust to shifting market demands.

These actual case studies show how companies in a range of sectors have effectively reduced expenses by implementing creative tactics and procedures. Through an emphasis on efficiency, waste reduction, technology adoption, and strategic alliances, firms can boost their competitive standing in the market and realize significant cost savings.

Employee Productivity

Businesses looking to enhance productivity, spur innovation, and keep a competitive advantage in the market must invest in employee productivity. The following are some essential ideas for funding worker productivity:

Education and Training:

Encouraging employees to participate in continuing education and training is essential for improving their performance, abilities, and knowledge. Putting money into workshops, certificates, and training programs gives staff members the skills and knowledge they need to flourish in their positions and add value to the company.

Worker Involvement:

Employees who are engaged are more dedicated, productive, and driven to meet company objectives. Putting money into employee engagement programs, team-building exercises, and frequent feedback sessions improves overall productivity and cultivates a happy work atmosphere.

Workplace Adjustment:

Allowing for flexibility in work arrangements—such as reduced workweeks, flexible hours, or remote work options—can increase worker productivity by fostering a work-life balance and taking into account individual requirements and preferences. Putting money into flexible workplace rules shows employees that you trust them and gives them the tools they need to manage their time well.

Tools and Technology:

Employees can operate more productively and efficiently when they have access to the newest tools, resources, and technology. Purchasing ergonomic equipment, productivity tools, and software solutions improves cooperation, automates tedious chores, and simplifies workflows—all of which contribute to higher productivity and innovation.

Wellness and Health Initiatives:

Performance and productivity are directly impacted by employee well-being. Putting money into health and wellness initiatives, such as gym memberships, mental health services, and workstations, encourages worker wellbeing, lowers absenteeism, boosts morale, and increases engagement and productivity.

Management of Performance:

Establishing strong performance management procedures and tools enables companies to identify and reward top performers, set clear goals, and offer frequent feedback. Investing in performance management increases productivity and outcomes by promoting accountability, promoting continuous development, and coordinating personal objectives with corporate goals.

Developing Leadership:

Promoting a high-performance culture and increasing staff productivity requires strong leadership. Putting money into coaching, mentorship, and leadership development programs produces successful leaders who can encourage, inspire, and enable their people to achieve success. Businesses may realize the full potential of their staff, propel organizational success, and achieve sustainable growth in the cutthroat business environment of today by adopting these ideas and investing in employee productivity.

Employee Training

Skills Development:

Training initiatives concentrate on fostering the development of particular abilities necessary for job duties and obligations. Targeted training makes people more confident and productive at work, whether it's through leadership skills for managerial jobs, customer service skills for roles involving clients, or technical abilities connected to software usage.

Productivity Tools:

Training courses give staff members access to tools and methods for maximizing time management, task prioritization, and teamwork. Employees can increase their productivity and efficiency in their daily jobs by learning how to properly use various technologies, such as task-tracking software, communication platforms, and project management software.

Regulatory and Compliance Training:

Training courses on laws, rules, and industry standards are crucial in industries with stringent regulations and compliance requirements. In addition to reducing risks, making sure staff members are aware of and follow compliance procedures promotes a culture of accountability and responsibility, which facilitates smoother operations and increased productivity.

On-the-Job Training and Mentorship:

Outside of official training courses, opportunities for on-the-job training and mentorship are essential for increasing productivity. By matching up new hires with seasoned mentors, performance and efficiency are eventually increased through practical learning, information transfer, and skill development in real-world situations. Staff training is essential to the success of an organization since it increases production, performance, and efficiency. Businesses can empower their people to perform at their best and reach their full potential by investing in comprehensive training programs that cover skill development, process familiarity, technology adoption, compliance, and continuous improvement.

Improving productivity and lowering errors with focused training is essential to raising organizational performance and efficiency. These kinds of training programs have a big impact because they sharpen employees' abilities and knowledge and give them the tools they need to do their jobs well. These courses focus on certain work activities or procedures, identifying typical mistake causes, and implementing a thorough awareness of best practices and error-prevention methods. By providing workers with this level of information, companies reduce errors and the resulting expenses and delays.

Moreover, focused training programs lead efforts to improve efficiency by locating and fixing inefficiencies in workflows and procedures. Workers receive effective procedures, time-saving strategies, and shortcuts, which provide streamlined operations, resource optimization, and increased productivity in general. This strategy also includes creating job-specific competencies that are adapted to the needs of different positions or duties inside the company. Targeted training makes sure staff members are competent in carrying out their responsibilities with accuracy and efficiency, whether they are learning software applications, perfecting machinery operation skills, or improving communication proficiencies.

Targeted training encourages employees to find areas for improvement and take the initiative to put solutions in place, which helps to foster a culture of continuous improvement. Organizations provide the conditions for gradual improvements in output and performance over time by promoting feedback channels, knowledge exchange, and continuing learning initiatives. Furthermore, these kinds of training programs are essential to risk reduction since they address issues related to errors, inconsistencies, or non-compliance. Employees who have received focused training are better equipped to negotiate possible risks, minimize disruptions, and strengthen organizational resilience.

Lastly, providing focused training opportunities demonstrates an organization's dedication to the advancement and professional development of its personnel. Providing opportunities for employees to broaden their skill sets and knowledge base helps firms cultivate a workforce that is highly engaged, loyal, and satisfied. Because they feel appreciated and involved, engaged workers are more likely to take responsibility for their work, aim for excellence, and make a positive contribution to the success and productivity of the company.

Eco-friendly Activities

Integrating environmentally friendly activities into corporate operations is a sustainable approach to cost reduction that benefits the environment at the same time.

Energy Efficiency:

You may save a lot of money on utility costs by putting energy-efficient practices into place, like buying energy-efficient equipment, employing LED lighting, and optimizing heating and cooling systems. Organizations can align with sustainability goals by lowering their operating expenses and carbon footprint through the reduction of energy consumption.

Waste Reduction and Recycling:

Implementing recycling and waste reduction initiatives can cut expenses associated with disposing of waste and provide income from recovered materials. Organizations can avoid waste from landfills, save disposal costs, and possibly make money from selling recyclable items by putting waste segregation into practice, composting organic waste, and recycling paper, plastic, and other materials.

Supply Chain Optimization:

By reducing transportation costs, enhancing inventory control, and using fewer packaging materials, supply chain procedures can be streamlined and eco-friendly suppliers can be partnered with to save money. Throughout the supply chain, companies can promote environmental responsibility and optimize costs by working with suppliers who are dedicated to sustainable practices.

Water Conservation:

Putting water-saving fixtures in place, setting up drip irrigation systems, and recycling wastewater are just a few examples of how conserving water can save a lot of money on water bills and wastewater treatment costs. Organizations can show their commitment to sustainability and preserve a key resource by lowering their water consumption.

Green Building Practices:

Long-term cost savings on construction, maintenance, and operating expenses can be achieved by investing in green building practices, such as sustainable materials, energy-efficient building design, and green certifications like LEED (Leadership in Energy and Environmental Design). Green buildings often use less energy, need fewer resources, and provide better indoor air quality, which reduces utility costs and increases worker happiness and productivity.

Evaluating the financial benefits of sustainability initiatives requires putting a number on the cost savings and revenue streams connected to green practices. Organizations can demonstrate the observable returns on investment from their sustainability efforts by carrying out cost-benefit analyses. Long-term revenue growth can also be achieved by emphasizing the beneficial social and environmental effects of sustainable practices, which can also improve brand reputation and draw in environmentally concerned customers.

Our discussion has emphasized how critical it is to put strategic ideas into action in order to promote sustainability, increase efficiency, and accelerate corporate growth. Organizations have a multitude of options to optimize operations and achieve long-term success, from utilizing focused training programs to lower errors and increase productivity to adopting sustainable practices for cost savings. Adopting these tactics will help organizations navigate a constantly changing environment and create a more sustainable, resilient, and efficient future for all.

12

Strategic Planning for Sustainable Growth

Any firm that wants to expand and succeed over the long run must keep its goals in mind and match its tactics with its financial goals. Businesses must look at their future and make decisions in the present to impact that future. Thus, long-term goals establish exactly those future goals. Businesses can lay out a plan for eventually reaching financial stability and profitability by defining specific long-term goals and creating methods to support them. Whether the goal is to grow market share, boost income, or improve shareholder value, matching strategies to financial targets guarantees that every choice and action advances the organization's overall goals. Establishing measurable metrics and key performance indicators (KPIs) to monitor progress toward their goals is a crucial part of matching plans with financial goals.

Starbucks KPIs and Sustainability

Starbucks is a global chain of coffee shops that exemplifies smart strategic planning with an emphasis on growing markets, improving customer satisfaction, and stimulating innovation. Starbucks increases the size of its global footprint by opening locations in rapidly developing nations like China and India and by making the most of its current locations in developed nations. The opening of new stores, are examples of key performance indicators (KPIs). Customer happiness, average transaction values, and frequency of visits are all increased by investments in technology such as smartphone ordering, barista training, and store improvements.

In addition, Starbucks is dedicated to sustainability by obtaining coffee that is produced responsibly, cutting waste by using recyclable materials, and making investments in renewable energy. Here, waste reduction goals, the percentage of coffee obtained ethically, and the use of sustainable energy are all KPIs. Revenue growth and consumer engagement are driven by ongoing innovations in products and services, such as new food and beverage offerings and distinctive shop formats like Starbucks Reserve Roasteries. KPIs include new product sales, customer satisfaction, and adoption of new retail formats. All things considered, Starbucks' strategic planning synchronizes objectives with KPIs, propelling expansion and cultivating innovation worldwide.

Amazon and KPIs

One of the biggest e-commerce and internet companies in the world, Amazon, has successfully used quantifiable measurements and key performance indicators (KPIs) to meet its objectives of sustaining high customer happiness and long-term growth. Amazon makes sure it meets and exceeds consumer expectations while boosting profitability by concentrating on particular KPIs. In order to put KPIs into practice, Amazon uses data analytics and real-time reporting to track performance as well as the collection and analysis of consumer input from surveys and reviews. Frequent performance reviews make it easier to spot trends and quickly resolve problems. Amazon has made significant investments in streamlining its delivery network and logistics to better guarantee on-time delivery while boosting effectiveness and cutting expenses.

Amazon Prime and similar programs increase customer retention by providing exclusive privileges that are regularly assessed based on input from customers. Consequently, Amazon continuously attains substantial revenue growth, robust operating margins, and high levels of customer happiness and loyalty. Amazon links its objectives with financial goals by methodically measuring and analyzing these KPIs, which promotes long-term performance.

Businesses can discover areas of strength and possibilities for progress by routinely tracking and analyzing performance against these indicators. This enables them to make the necessary, timely adjustments to tactics.

Furthermore, using sound financial management techniques like forecasting, budgeting, and risk management is necessary to match current goals with financial objectives. Through resource allocation, effective cash flow management, and proactive risk mitigation, businesses may protect their financial well-being and set themselves up for success. Additionally, companies need to give priority to funding projects that result in value development and yield profits. This could entail making investments in R&D, breaking into new markets, or improving operational effectiveness in order to gradually increase revenue and profitability.

When aligning plans with financial goals, firms should also take into account the influence of external factors, such as market developments, regulatory changes, and economic situations. Businesses can effectively traverse hurdles and capitalize on new opportunities to reach their objectives by remaining aware of external dynamics and adjusting their plans accordingly.

The alignment of plans with financial objectives is a crucial aspect of decision-making, performance enhancement, and the maintenance of business operations sustainability. Businesses can position themselves for development, profitability, and success in the ever-evolving business landscape by concentrating on long-term goals, developing clear benchmarks for success, and implementing responsible financial management procedures.

It takes a complete structure that combines financial planning, performance evaluation, and decision-making to further ensure that business goals are in line with its financial goals. The following are some ways that organizations might improve the alignment between their financial goals and strategies:

Fiscal Forecasting and Budgeting:

Create accurate financial forecasts and budgets that take into account the future goals and aspirations of the company. Businesses may effectively manage resources, detect potential financing shortfalls, and guarantee that financial resources are allocated to programs that yield the highest value by coordinating with financial predictions.

Cost Management and Efficiency:

Maintaining quality and performance standards while reducing costs and increasing efficiency should be the top priorities when implementing cost management techniques. To find areas of waste, inefficiency, or overpaying, do an in-depth cost analysis. Then, put strategies in place to optimize costs throughout the company.

Revenue Growth:

Create revenue growth plans that complement the organization's financial objectives. Diversifying revenue streams and lessening dependency on any one source of income may entail entering new markets, introducing new goods or services, improving attempts to retain customers, or expanding into new areas.

Risk Management:

Reduce any monetary risks that can hinder the accomplishment of goals. To reduce the impact of prospective risks on financial performance, such as market volatility, regulatory changes, or competitive challenges, identify them and adopt risk management solutions. To guard against unfavorable occurrences, this may include putting insurance policies, hedging techniques, or backup plans into action.

Performance Measurement and Monitoring:

Determine metrics and key performance indicators (KPIs) to monitor the success of initiatives and gauge progress made toward financial goals. Maintain alignment by routinely tracking and evaluating financial performance in relation to KPIs, and implementing measures as needed.

Adaptability and Flexibility:

To effectively respond to shifting market conditions, consumer preferences, and industry trends, keep your business strategy flexible. It is imperative to periodically review and modify tactics in light of fresh data, input, and developing prospects in order to maximize financial outcomes and promote expansion.

By using these tactics, businesses can better the alignment of their financial goals with their company goals, which will ultimately lead to increased profitability, success, and financial performance.

In the business world, sustainability refers to achieving current goals without endangering the capacity of future generations to achieve their own goals. Sustainability in the social, environmental, and economic spheres are its three foundations. Reducing carbon emissions, conserving resources, and using green technologies are some of the ways that environmental sustainability aims to minimize the effects of company operations on the environment. The main goals of social sustainability are to support community projects, guarantee safe working conditions, and encourage equitable treatment of employees. The goal of economic sustainability is to sustain long-term profitability via inventiveness, responsible financial management, and moral business conduct.

Enterprises that include sustainability in their fundamental approaches can limit expenses, alleviate hazards, and foster adaptability. Additionally, they draw talent, investors, and customers who value social and environmental responsibility. In the corporate world, sustainability is not only a duty; it's also a chance to add value, build credibility, and help ensure a more prosperous future.

Maintaining the continuous performance of firms requires striking a balance between short-term benefits and long-term sustainability. Here's how businesses can successfully strike this balance:

Planning:

Create a thorough plan that integrates sustainability goals with short-term targets. This should include precise steps and activities to attain immediate benefits while also taking the organization's long-term picture into account.

Transparency and Reporting:

Continue to be transparent when disclosing information about long-term objectives and financial performance. Organizations may establish credibility and confidence among shareholders and show their dedication to ethical business practices by being transparent with them regarding the trade-offs between short- and long-term sustainability.

Continuous Improvement:

Constantly assess how actions made in the short-term affect the business in the long run and modify plans and procedures accordingly.

Organizations can minimize risks and adverse effects on shareholders and the environment while maximizing value creation by finding a balance between short-term benefits and long-term sustainability. By using a comprehensive approach to decision-making, companies may be flexible, strong, and well-positioned for success despite changing opportunities and difficulties.

Scenario Planning

Scenario planning is essential in today's fast-paced business world to ensure readiness for unforeseen circumstances. Businesses need to be ready for a variety of eventualities that can interfere with operations or have an adverse effect on their capacity to maintain financial stability. Businesses should proactively establish plans to prevent negative consequences and benefit from new trends by recognizing significant risks and opportunities. In scenario planning, multiple possible futures are evaluated, taking into account variables like changes in the economy, technology, laws, and geopolitical unrest. Organizations may make educated decisions and take proactive measures to minimize the impact of unforeseen events by utilizing this method, which provides them with important insights into prospective challenges and possibilities.

Shell and Scenario Planning

The multinational oil and petrochemical corporation Shell is well-known for using scenario planning a lot. Shell employs scenario planning as a means of navigating the ever-changing geopolitical landscape, shifting economic conditions, and environmental restrictions that impact the global energy market. Shell is able to make well-informed strategic decisions and better prepare for a range of outcomes by creating many scenarios that depict different possible futures.

For example, Shell was able to predict how changes in oil prices and geopolitical unrest would affect their business operations because of their scenario planning. Because of this foresight, Shell is able to adapt its investments in exploration, production, and renewable energy sources in a way that ensures sustainability in a dynamic market. Shell has benefited greatly from scenario planning, which has allowed them to adapt and prosper in a constantly shifting global environment.

Making the least amount of disturbance possible in the event of an unexpected incident is one of the main goals of scenario preparation. Organizations can create backup plans and effective reaction techniques to deal with pressing issues quickly by imagining many scenarios and their possible effects. Businesses can find weaknesses, improve operational strength, and deploy resources to reduce risks. Through scenario planning, businesses may better prepare for unforeseen events and negotiate uncertainty with confidence and agility. Examples of this include diversifying supply chains, upgrading cybersecurity processes, and putting business continuity plans into place.

Furthermore, scenario planning encourages an innovative and flexible culture in businesses. Scenario planning fosters creativity and problem-solving abilities by pushing shareholders to consider future possibilities and consider alternate options. Teams are more equipped to foresee change, spot development possibilities, and adjust plans of action as necessary to keep ahead of changing market conditions thanks to this collaborative approach. Moreover, scenario planning improves organizational learning and agility, allowing companies to take advantage of new opportunities, adapt quickly to unforeseen circumstances, and maintain success in a turbulent and complicated business environment.

Scenario planning for preparedness is a critical need for companies looking to prosper in an unpredictable environment. Organizations may become stronger in the face of adversity by increasing their capacity to withstand storms, reduce risks, and take advantage of opportunities by predicting possible obstacles and promoting adaptation. Businesses can set themselves up for success by proactively planning for scenarios, which will ensure development and continuity in a constantly shifting business environment.

In today's dynamic business world, it is critical to create flexible company plans that can be adjusted to changing market conditions. Organizations that are flexible may efficiently manage risks, take advantage of new possibilities, and react quickly to changing market trends. An agile framework that puts flexibility and iteration ahead of strict objectives is the foundation of flexible business planning. With this, companies can stay ahead of the curve by constantly evaluating the state of the industry, client demands, and competition dynamics and modifying their approach accordingly.

Another essential element of adaptable business plans is modular planning. Organizations can modify particular elements of their strategy, such as product offers, marketing, or distribution routes, without having to completely rework the plan when they divide plans into modular components.

Lego and Modular Planning

The well-known Danish toy business Lego is a prime example of modular planning in both market strategy and product development. Lego uses a modular design process for its toys, meaning that different buildings may be created by combining components in different ways.

In addition to increasing play value and inventiveness, Lego sets' modular architecture makes it simple to add to or alter them over time.

Lego uses modular planning as a commercial model by creating themed sets that can be combined into bigger collections. Lego is able to satisfy a wide range of consumer interests while upholding a consistent brand identity thanks to this strategy. Lego effectively responds to consumer tastes and market trends by introducing new sets and themes on a regular basis through the use of modular planning. Lego's global success and popularity have been sustained in large part due to its flexibility.

Another essential component of encouraging adaptability and agility in corporate planning is cross-functional cooperation. Organizations are better able to quickly respond to changes in the market by leveraging varied viewpoints and skills by dismantling departmental and team silos and fostering collaboration. This cooperative strategy makes it possible for smooth communication, coordination, and alignment, which promotes quick decision-making and implementation.

Measurement and Analysis of Financial Gains

One of the most important components of flexible business planning and market adaptability is the measurement and analysis of financial gains. It entails putting a monetary value on strategic choices and endeavors in order to assess their effectiveness and direct subsequent activities. Organizations can obtain important insights into their financial performance and make well-informed plan revisions by utilizing a variety of analytical techniques and measures.

Measuring financial gains starts with establishing essential financial performance metrics. A comprehensive view of the organization's financial health and the effectiveness of its plans can be obtained by metrics including cash flow, profitability, revenue growth, and return on investment (ROI). Businesses can assess their progress toward financial goals and pinpoint opportunities for improvement by routinely reviewing these measures.

A further useful method for evaluating financial gains is comparative analysis. Organizations can learn more about their relative position in the market by comparing their financial performance to that of competitors, peers in the industry, or historical data. In addition to providing context for understanding financial results, this analysis aids in identifying strengths and shortcomings. When determining if investments or initiatives are financially viable, cost-benefit analysis is an essential tool. Businesses can allocate resources wisely and give priority to projects with the greatest potential for financial gain by comparing the expenses of a given plan to its anticipated benefits or returns.

Organizations may track financial performance and spot patterns or abnormalities as soon as they appear with the use of real-time data analysis. Businesses can identify chances for optimization or intervention early on and take proactive steps to capitalize on opportunities or reduce risks by using real-time financial data analysis. Financial gains must be measured and analyzed in order to inform decisions, assess the efficacy of various tactics, and promote ongoing development. Organizations can optimize financial advantages and achieve success by utilizing a variety of analytical tools and approaches to get important insights into their financial performance and make informed decisions.

Netflix and Real-time Data Analysis

Real-time data analysis is a key component used by Netflix, a well-known streaming service, to improve user experience and streamline content delivery. In order to make data-driven decisions, Netflix continuously tracks viewer behavior, preferences, and engagement patterns through advanced analytics. Netflix is able to tailor content recommendations depending on individual viewing behaviors thanks to this real-time data analysis. Netflix is able to provide each user with personalized recommendations for movies and TV series in real time by monitoring viewer activities, including clicks, searches, and viewing duration. This tailored approach raises platform-wide content consumption while also enhancing user happiness.

For instance, the Netflix platform analyzes a user's watching history and interactions in real-time when they log in. Netflix suggests material that matches the interests of its users on the homepage through personalized recommendations that are generated based on this data. With a highly customized user experience, Netflix's real-time content recommendation system helps keep users.

Additionally, Netflix optimizes content generation and purchase decisions with real-time data. Netflix may allocate resources to creating or acquiring material that is likely to draw in and keep members by examining the kinds of content that users are most interested in watching at any particular moment. By utilizing data-driven insights to continuously improve user pleasure and engagement, Netflix has been able to sustain its leadership position in the streaming business. This has been made possible by the application of real-time data analysis.

As We End

Organizations may efficiently manage risks, take advantage of opportunities, and adjust to shifting market conditions by using flexible business plans and scenario planning. In order to increase productivity and drive efficiency, we also must look at the need to utilize customer retention techniques, cut operational expenses, and invest in staff development. Businesses can improve their competitiveness by placing a higher priority on staff development, cost reduction, and customer connections.

We also talked about how important it is to measure and analyze financial gains since it helps firms assess the success of their strategy and make data-driven decisions that maximize performance. As we come to an end, I urge readers to implement the tactics we've covered in their own work environments, customizing them to fit their own objectives and special situations. Businesses may manage obstacles, seize opportunities, and create prosperity for the business by adopting an innovative, agile, and continuous improvement approach.

Thus, building wealth involves more than just being financially successful; it also involves adding value for all parties involved, giving back to the community, and leaving a lasting legacy for future generations. Businesses can steer toward success and have a significant impact on the globe by adopting the ideas discussed.

The tactics mentioned find strong support and inspiration from real-world success stories and testimonials from businesses that have earned growth through incremental gains. These tales demonstrate how gradual, minor adjustments made over time can result in considerable achievement and financial gain. Here are a few instances:

The outdoor clothing brand Patagonia, which is renowned for its dedication to environmental sustainability, is one example of such a success story. Patagonia has steadily grown and been profitable by putting quality before quantity, adopting eco-friendly procedures, and cultivating a devoted consumer base. Their emphasis on sustainability has helped them stand out from the competition and connect with customers who care about the environment, which has increased sales and brand loyalty.

Costco, a warehouse store with a membership model, is another example. The core of Costco's business strategy is to offer its members high-quality goods at competitive costs while also putting staff welfare and customer pleasure first. Costco has become one of the biggest retailers in the world by achieving growth and profitability through a combination of effective management, bulk purchasing, and a devoted membership base.

Furthermore, by providing fashionable, reasonably priced spectacles online, the eyeglasses brand Warby Parker has upended the established eyewear market. Through direct sales to customers, Warby Parker has eliminated intermediaries and is able to provide premium eyeglasses at a significantly lower price than traditional stores. They have achieved success and profitability because of their creative business ideas and significant emphasis on customer satisfaction and social responsibility.

These success stories show how deliberate decision-making and steady gains may be used to create wealth that lasts. Businesses may achieve long-term success and positively impact their sectors and communities by embracing innovation, investing in customer connections, and prioritizing long-term goals. These testimonies demonstrate that wealth is about more than just making money; it's also about leaving a lasting legacy for future generations, and producing value.

Conclusion

What better way is there to conclude this writing than to review where we have been on our journey? What more important topic can we select in the business world than that of profits? Let's think back for a moment to Chapter 8 and all the ways in which revenues might be developed to create new highs in sales. Recall how we discussed rebranding your products, followed by creating new products. We looked next to the direct costs of materials and direct labor that gave us the products to sell for healthy profit margins.

Finally, we turned our attention to the operating expenses that support our sales and costs. Operating Expenses such as rent, utilities, and transportation, that is, all expense categories that are required to place our completed products into the hands of consumers, resulting in profits being earned.

We recognized the importance of each step taken along the path to selling and earning profits. We learned the value of focusing our attention on each step, with the goal of maximizing our results. Examples were given of actual successful industry giants that can show us the way, they have shown us proven methods of monitoring and testing that will assist us in reaching long-term goals in our own companies.

We introduced the concept of the micro-profit Committee, designed to provide support in our organization to improve company profits.

We have totally embraced the concepts of Micro-profiting, placed them into action, and look forward to the results. We sincerely hope that you have found new ideas and concepts in this book that will be a guide in building your company to new heights in sales and profits!

www.ingramcontent.com/pod-product-compliance
Lightning Source LLC
LaVergne TN
LVHW050937210926
848482LV00013B/652
9798896690061